ARRIVAL PRESS

Picture This

With all my love
Iris.
12/97.

Edited by Tim Sharp

ARRIVAL PRESS

Picture This

Recreating the Poetry Tradition

First published in Great Britain in 1997 by

ARRIVAL PRESS
1-2 Wainman Road, Woodston,
Peterborough, PE2 7BU
Telephone (01733) 230762

HB ISBN 1 85786 690 8
SB ISBN 1 85786 685 1

Foreword

A photograph is the perfect way to capture a special moment, just as a poem is the perfect way to capture your thoughts. So, what better way to relive your fondest memories, than with a photo and poem that go hand in hand.

The poets in this anthology have come from all walks of life, to share with the reader, the story behind a favourite picutre. Whether humorous, touching, or just plain nonsense, they were all inspired to put pen to paper by a particular photo that is special to them.

This should make for a hugely entertaining and enlightening read, providing an insight into the minds and memories of poets from around the country.

Tim Sharp
Editor

Contents

The Poems

Poet's vision for Year 2000

POOLE writer Desmond Tarrant has published a major new poem which offers a "Holy Grail" for the 21st Century – a new vision of science and spirituality.

In SUNSET OR SUNRISE?" or PARADISE FOUND (Aural Images, £1.50), Mr Tarrant seeks to "use science imaginatively as the basis of a new spiritual synthesis".

His standpoint is that science needn't preclude spirituality – indeed, thatwe can find spirituality THROUGH science.

"Have we in this age of stratospheric
Flight so lost the gift of sight, in cloudy
Night to be entangled, from

Desmond Tarrant

the cheering
Mighty roar of Heaven's light quite cut off?

The poem, he says, "helps to ring down the curtain on a century of short-sighted and pessimistic realism".

He has a vision of "a new Romantic Renaissance, ushering in the 21st Century as Wordsworth and Coleridge ushered in 19th Century Romanticism in 1798".

In his foreward to the work, the late author and educationalist Sir George Trevelyan declares that Sunset or Sunrise? lifted him "with mystery and delight".

Now in his 70s, Mr Tarrant is a respected intellectual and academic who has lectured and researched at many colleges and universities in Britain and in America. He also has a distinguished war record.

■ Sunset or Sunrise? or Paradise Found by Desmond Tarrant is available from Aural Images, 5, Hamilton Street, Astley Bridge, Bolton BL1 6RJ (tel 01204 596369). The price, including postage, is £1.75.

Mating Call

What though our Spring of love be over?
Its flow is channelled now less wastefully,
A torrent nonetheless of surging force
Because perforce its course is more direct.

As your gaze becomes bereft of shallows
That once did harm as well as charm the hull,
The undercurrents sweeping all along
Echo a song stirring much more deeply.

Now hurt in words comes not from a heart
Whose part is played in tune, fully rounded
With the golden ring of summer's welkin -
As pots and pans with children chime their rimes.

In open verse this mating call is all
That purse strings ever buy that in the end
The moments spend without the costly lie
That flies to strip our summer's sheen and mar
The fall of autumn's raiment, leaving bare,
Lamenting, winter's shriven discontent.

Seeded in those moments bought with rapids
Fought, the foaming shoals treacherous till the
Sea was almost lost in tearful spray, like
Mists that cloud the azure eyes of Helen,
Is this call. Still must it incorporate
Love's thrall in the heavenly halls of your embrace -
As does this hull emblaze with gazing on your face.

Desmond Tarrant

New Beginnings

As Mary gazed into his eyes
With love so pure and true
Her heart was breaking full of pain
Because she knew what he must do.

He lifted his eyes to see her face
His hood dripping with blood and tears
'Oh dear mother I love you so
Do not hold back your tears.'

When at last it was all down
And darkness was all around
All of a sudden thunder and rain
And lightning covered the ground

The earth opened up and gave
Up its dead and all hell was
Let loose on that day.
When our dear Lord was crucified
All they could do was to pray

Jesus appeared to Mary as she
Was walking towards the tomb
Why are you weeping my dear child
I have come back to you

Jesus appeared many times to all his
Friends he knew as he was being taken
He said I will come back to you.

K P Wiseman

The Bouncers

(With my humblest apologies to Shakespeare!)

First bouncer	When shall we three meet again, to inflict torment and pain?
Second bouncer	When the disco's just begun - that's when we shall have *our* fun.
Third bouncer	That will be past set of sun . . .
First bouncer	Where the action?
Second bouncer	At Blackheath, on the door of Frankie's Club -
Third bouncer	There to meet . . . e'en death.

Sue Millward

Winter's Theatre

The air is cold
But I'm warm inside
When I see the sun glisten
On the winter's tide.

The unclothed cedars
Bow to the sea
And hum sweet melodies
To their audience - just me.

The sun disappears
Behind tempestuous cloud
And snow veils the scene
In a pure white shroud.

The songs continue
From trees, wind and sea
Reaching a crescendo
For their audience - just me.

Jenny L Treacher

Terra Astra

Watch for doors and inroads
where the wild realm meets the sky
where lies the next dimension
where the wings of fancy fly
some lie in the forest
waiting for a key
waiting for a brave soul
to cross the boundary

Walk on silent feet now
the way is very near
the key is there for taking
listen, can you hear
songs of Terra Astra
molten, like desire
weaving through the birches
woodwind, voice and lyre

A new dimension beckons
wraps its fingers round your heart
in the dappled shadows
the bushes move apart
feel their eyes upon you
as you enter their domain
they're reaching out with arms and paws
to greet you home again.

Sara Russell

Grandad's Ride

Grandad will you please let go
Don't be scared, I'm not you know
Going up, way up to the sky
Really exciting, my tummy's all butterflies

Grandad, you don't look so good
Oh dear! I think your dinner's got loose
The swings go higher, faster too
Goodness me! There goes your stew

Oh! Poor Grandad, you look so green
This ride? Don't think you're so keen
It's slowing down, almost stopped
Grandad's face has surely dropped

Very shakey as he alights
Another go Grandad
Huh, not on your life?

Patricia J Smith

Dreams Are Made Of This

In my life I've tried to achieve,
we all have hidden talents, I've dreamed of many things
I've entered competitions, done bingo, the
Lottery, but alas only had small wins.

I've done a bit of modelling work,
sang with singers on stage, and in a bar.
My dreams were met on many occasions
I was nervous once, now a local star.

People tell me I resemble Cher,
As her I would be right on cue.
I'd not only buy my flat, but a dream
House abroad with fantastic view.

I achieved social welfare, and have
worked with children doing an NVQ.
Life's a balancing act, we move on, now
I'm with the elderly, enjoying what I do.

Writing poetry now gives me pleasure
in this I've fulfilled a desire.
Another is to meet the man of my dreams,
Who'd set my heart on fire.

M Jowsey

Contentment

Contentment is the joy of a bright summer's day,
It is the sweet song of birds, the perfume of flowers,
The merry laughter of children at play.
The tranquillity in the face of the old,
It is the glow that warms the heart,
Seeing the happiness of others unfold.
It is the glory of the thrill of fine music.
The gentle peace of a golden sunset,
It is the benediction of a hallowed building,
The stillness at the end of a day, well spent.

Margaret White

Where In The World

Did I climb mountains
in the Himalayas
seeking to touch the
roof of the world?
Or, was this an island
uninhabited by man
waiting for my footsteps
in the sand?

Did I charter a spaceship
to the moon
following those exalted
steps for mankind?
Or, did I swim beneath
the sea, exploring
hidden fishy depths
in Davy Jones' Locker?

No, not so far from home
but no less enthralling
in its wondrous landscape.
Ilfracombe, pride of North Devon.
Strange, awe inspiring, hunchback
rocks appearing through sea murk,
peaceful tranquillity lifting
the soul to levels beyond
the green seaweed
and grey swirling mist.
No far flung land
or watery depths
could have restored my faith
as did that mysterious English cove.

Maisie Dance

What I See

I can't deny the beauty and power I see
and feel looking at the sky with the clouds speeding
by the power to move them must come from heaven high
I can't deny the beauty I see the leaves on the trees
now turning red the grass always green what thought
with care went into it all was it man made no heaven sent.

R P Scannell

Return Of Childhood

If only childhood could return
When snow was on the ground,
When white and blue were splashed by light
And morning hush was found.
When footsteps, soft along the way
All trees wore ermine dress,
When all was fresh and clean, renewed
And cares grew less and less.
Then romp within this rural scene
To smile and laugh with others,
Unknowing of all worldly woes
That joy in adults smothers.

To cast a frozen ball of snow
At targets' random choice
And strike a branch of snowbound tree
Then shout in child's high voice.

To make a snowman, undisturbed
In magic world, so soft,
And feel creation's flowing joy
While glancing high aloft;
In hope that only snow would fall
Not rain to blight your day
To further beautify your world
Just made for you to play.

Then childhood can be born again
Through mind's deep hidden sight,
And you may sit by comfort's fire
And turn your grey world white.

Henry J Green

The Wedding

It's now 44 years since we said 'I do'
For all the happiness we have shared - my thanks go to you
On the Anniversary of D Day in Coronation week we were wed
June 6th 1953 when our vows were said.

Life has not been easy and tears have been shed too
But we knew from the start life was up to me and you
We have had our ups and downs but we have come through
Blessed with Paul Helen and Mark our family grew.

Taken all round life has been good to you and me
And now we have four grandchildren to complete our family
I'm so happy my darling that you chose me
From your loving wife Marjorie.

Marjorie Ridley

Emmy Lou

(Aged two and a bit and holding!)

She has red, rosy rounded cheeks,
Her hair is akin to pump water
From her sparkling brown eyes
Shines good humour, love and
Mischief.
She wants to play with the big
Girls and sometimes can't quite
Keep up.
She is still too fast for failing, ailing
Grandparents who faint at
The speed she moves.
Her dance when she sees us
Has the grace of a cygnet, and
The warm clasp around the knees
Leaves marks on clothes to die for . . .
No matter, when she loves us so much.
Her little world revolves around her family.
She is Daddy's girl, Mummy's companion
A little sister, a big cousin.
A total menace in the bath and enchanting when
Tucked up safely in bed.
We all love you Emma Louise.

Hilary Moore

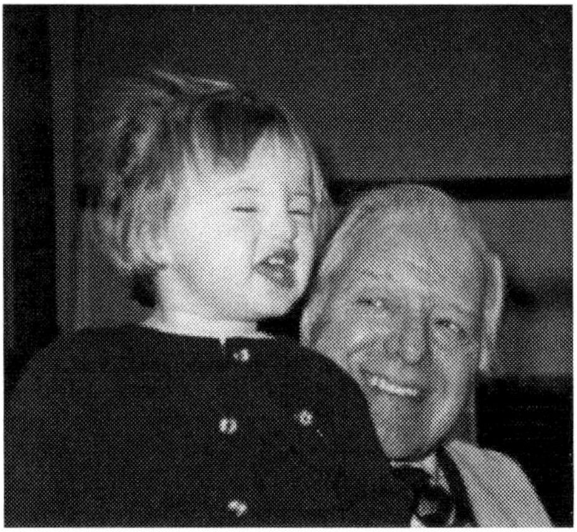

The Sea

I love to walk down by the sea
And to feel the foamy mist,
It's the only way to be free
And forget the way we kissed

I love to watch the waves
Crashing to the banks
I know our love it will not save
But still I give it thanks

I love to feel the breeze
Blow gently through my hair
And for a little while
I have not a single care

I know you never will come back
Though you are still alive
But with my love of the sea
I know I will survive

Janet Larkin

The Sunshine Of Your Smile

We sit at our window, my hubby and I,
We sit and watch the world go by.
And if someone waves, and gives a smile
It makes the rest of our day worthwhile.
We're disabled you see, and can't get about,
Unless someone gives us the chance to get out.
And, oh! What a treat to leave these four walls,
Just sitting, and hoping, that somebody calls.
We look safe, and happy, to those outside,
But they don't know the loneliness we both hide.
We've a wonderful family, ready to give,
But we must not forget they have their lives to live.
We were once young, and busy as they,
And never once thought of the old, and gray.
So, not complaining, but wanted to say,
Just smile at the old, and you'll make their day.

Sylvia M Needham

Who's The Boss?

I used to be boss in my own little home,
Queen of the castle I was.
Now all that has changed and what is the cause?
Brown eyes and a waggly tail.
I used to go for a leisurely walk,
Meeting people and stopping to talk.
Now I'm dragged along at a cracking pace,
With an anxious smile on my face,
As I try to tell myself I'm in control,
Knowing full well that I'm not.
For my four-legged friend has chosen the way,
I just walk to heel and obey.
There are doggie toys scattered all over the floor,
A half eaten chew on the mat,
She barks at the postman and chases the cat,
And leaps like a frog up the door.
She gets so excited when visitors call,
Circling around in the hall,
She tosses a worn-out old shoe at their feet,
In a welcome that's so hard to beat.
At the end of the day she jumps on my bed,
Snuggling down with a sigh,
And before I sleep I thank God on high,
For a friendship that money can't buy.
For my Sheba to me is more precious than gold,
A treasure not bought nor sold,
And she rules the roost but I hasten to say
I would have things no other way.

Jenny Porteous

Bluebell Wood

I remember how we stood
On that day in Bluebell Wood
And the world was calm,
The grass was never greener
The air seemed so much cleaner
No cause for alarm.

Bluebells like a picture sweet
Spread a carpet at our feet
Colour everywhere,
Yes, those days are locked in time
Precious days of yours and mine
Fragrance filled the air.

Was there ever shade of blue
Concentrated in one view!
Birds sang overhead,
All around a sense of fey
As we stood there on that day
By a Bluebell bed.

Then the trees shut out the sun
And the day was nearly done
All the world stood still,
I remember how we stood
On that day in Bluebell Wood
And I always will.

Moon and stars all brightly gleamed
On that wood wherein we dreamed
May the dream come true!
Aura of transcendent love
Which was ours all else above
Old, yet ever new.

Moira Wiggins

Goodbye To The Farm

I'll miss the morning chorus of the bird song,
and the sweet smell of new mown hay,
the gentle summer rain upon the meadow,
because for Me this is the parting of the way.

So goodbye Lilley's farm, goodbye to the land,
My heart is filled with sadness as I leave you,
goodbye Hutch, goodbye my many friends,
I'll not pass by, but long to be there too.

I'll never forget the pleasant hours I spent,
pulling wurzels, hoeing weeds and stooking corn,
and I'll remember too, my friends the bullocks,
just as we fed them in the early morn.

The work was hard and often very dirty,
we toiled in snow and sleet, bitter winds and rain,
but I'll remember the barn with warm log fire,
when I let my thoughts fly back again.

Though memory fades with passing time,
and fickle mind so quickly forgets,
in my lonely hours I will wander back,
to those happy times with no regrets.

Pamela Eckhardt

A Special Place

Down by the bridge, where the rippling stream
Gently meandered through bluebell woods,
When sunlight filtered the willow boughs
And birdsong floated on crystal air,
There we would meet, my love and I,
Counting each hour of our stolen days.
Enchanted in this special place
We banished the cruel world beyond;
It couldn't touch us there, we thought,
With all its narrow bigotry,
Nor force us to accept the truth
That, in our hearts, we always knew.

All summer long we hid ourselves away,
Treasuring each moment of our borrowed time;
Knowing that only in this special place
Could such a love as ours be safely shared.
But winter came and sunlight turned to storm,
The birds no longer sang, and love grew cold;
The disapproving world had crowded in
And spoiled the magic of our special place.
He said we always knew it had to end,
That nothing is forever in this life;
But still, for me, our special place remains
A poignant memory of that summer love.

J Scott

The Swan

My camera ready to click
But Mrs Swan was far too quick
She just wouldn't face the camera
No matter how I tried to coax her
She turned her back as if to say
There's better things to do today
I'll make ripples in the water for you to see
She did it with such dignity
Her wings she spread, upright she stood
This beautiful swan, facing the wood
Then she swam to her destiny
Imprinting this picture on my memory

Gladys C'Ailceta

The Guest

We had a charming little guest,
Who loved to mingle with the rest,
He sometimes sat on people's laps,
Whilst eating up those surplus scraps,
He sipped fresh milk, ate tender meats,
But rejected fancy sweets,
Our guest arrived without a car,
And never wandered very far,
We called him Tim, it was a shame
We did not know his proper name.
He accepted all, without a fee,
Enjoyed the hospitality.
When folk were ready to retire
The cat lay slumbering by the fire.

Mary Brassington

His Car

Here it is his pride and joy,
undoubtedly his favourite toy.
The fuss he makes of that bit of tin on wheels,
only another addict could know how he feels
The slightest squeak is pain to his ear
conjuring up some mechanical fear
A small scratch will drive him spare
always shouting at the kids, 'Hey don't play by there'
You can bet every Sunday if dry without fail
He'll be out there with his yellow sponge and pail
Determined to get 'his' the cleanest in the street
mind you he would be very hard to beat
Then when it's all nice, dry, and clean
He rubs on the polish to get a nice sheen
The inside gets a spring clean too
upholstery shampooed till it looks like new
The ashtrays emptied, all sweet papers gone
Even washes the mats we put our feet on
When finished and admiring his work
on his face he wears a self approval smirk
If only we could have just half the attention
he spends on his jalopy, with its perfect suspension
That car is the treasure of his life
alas we're just his kids and 'the wife'.

June Abbott

Christmas In Castletown

A moonlit night, a starry sky,
A tree stands proud with lights so high,
For it's Christmas in Castletown.

No snowflakes fall on steeples tall,
No Cinderella going to a ball,
When it's Christmas in Castletown.

Castle Rushen stands so proud all year,
But especially now, when Santa's here.
Yes it's Christmas in Castletown.

Like Fairyland the street lights shimmer,
On the harbour waters they dazzle and glimmer,
At Christmas in Castletown.

Happy faces rosy and bright,
Carol singers, brass bands, they sound through the night,
Now it's Christmas in Castletown.

The sea blows rough, it may even storm,
But the streets glow bright, they look cosy and warm,
This Christmas in Castletown.

Everyone's happy and full of good cheer.
For it's Christmas in Castletown
and I'm glad to be here!

Eileen Harper

The Skeleton Remains

This place - these shallow outlines.
The skeleton remains.
Echoes of past lives - each different
yet so alike in many ways.
Summoned by the 7.30am hooter -
dismissed at 5 o'clock by the same.
Blasting the cliff face - no safety here
except perhaps in numbers.
The red-hot kilns waiting,
like fiery dragons - mouths wide open,
greedy to swallow the bricks
moulded from the dusty grounded stone.
Billy-cans ready to brew the tea.
The tobacco tins appear - each rolls his own.
Coughing and spluttering - partly clearing the settling dust
from already damaged frames.
The weary choir sings its way
along the winding path home.

Iona James

Trees

There's nothing else that speaks to me
In tones so moving as a tree;
That stands between the earth and sky
A symbol of true majesty.

And from its roots, where time hath trod
It rises stately from the clod;
While in its leaves, where sunbeams rest,
The birds find shelter for their nest.

Around its girth is many a scar
That seeks its beauty thus to mar;
That tells of storm, of strain and stress
Through which it passed, the world to bless.

And as I stand it speaks to me
Of one who died upon a tree;
Whose visage was so deeply marred
Whose hands and feet were hurt and scarred.

Who sank at last into the clod,
The holy, spotless Son of God;
Then rose triumphant to the sky
And lives - that we need never die.

Laburnum's tints of hanging gold
Declare His glory, all untold;
While every blossom on the bough
Proclaims His praise, - in glory now.

And in a day that's yet to be,
He will return for all to see
And in His kingdom bright and fair
The tree of life, her fruits will bear.

Edna M Reading

Tina

(Leaving Home)

We knew one day you'd leave us
And we'd have to let you go
But please don't stay away too long
You know we love you so

There'll always be a place for you
Right here where you belong
Don't hesitate to come back home
If anything goes wrong

We know you have decided
And we cannot change your mind
But remember all the people
That you're leaving here behind

They all think the world of you
Yes! Just like me and dad
The thought of you not being here
Is making us feel sad.

Things will be so different here
Your room will be so bare
We'd rather that your clothes and things
Were scattered everywhere.

We're going to miss your smiling face
And all your little ways
And pray you'll soon come home again
And this is just a phase

Please don't forget your mum and dad
And always keep in touch
And Tina come and see us soon
We love you very much.

P R Simmons

My Sister

Who would know looking at you
What went on, what you've been through
A picture of beauty is what they see
But deep inside - it's a prison to thee
Who could guess - the scar lies within
Battling the fear, keeping it in
Refusing to surface those days of before
Refusing to open that now rusted door
Those days were quite, repression lay deep
I heard you once, alone you did weep
You hid childhood memories deep down inside
But not from me - for I also had cried
And who would know looking at you
The battle you fought the secret you knew
The difference now, that you have let go
To childhood memories which hurt you so
There's a person much stronger, wiser and free
A person who'll conquer all that will be
A picture of beauty, for now that you know
how much better it is, if we just let go.

Fiona Gilpin

The Village Church

I'd glimpsed the old church
many times
Intent on country walks;
Then one day a different aspect
Across the barley stalks;
Made me really notice where
That needle spire pierced the air.

When village life
Had been more slow,
This was its centre
Long ago.

Now it sees a different kind
Of life within its view
Busy traffic, huge machines
That harvest quickly too.

And yet within those ancient walls
Still quiet now as then recalls.
Man is no different deep within
His needs, his greeds,
His creeds, his sin
And God's forgiveness always there;
Who seek peace in this house of prayer.

J Facchini

Autumn Collection

What fool decreed that we should need to follow fashion?
See how my naked limbs tremble with the cold.
The nights grow longer, the garments, shorter,
The fabric finer, oh bad designer,
Bring back the frills, discard the gold.

This flimsy lace, will surely grace,
But never keep me warm.
See how the breeze wafts the sleeves round my waist;
And silver lamé is over the top:
It glitters well, but it just won't sell:
Bad sense, bad timing, bad taste.

Cherry Tompsett

Damien

You're my treasure
And I love you
I call you my big lad, and little man too.
Your smile and your face
You look just like your dad
Your dad was my brother Chris
Whom I sadly lost last year
Along with your mum
I shed many a tear
But you make me happy again
You keep your dad in my life
I'm your aunty and I love you Damien
For the rest of my life.

Heather Dunn-Fox from Leek

Magic Of Words

My exuberance of poetry writing
Comes from within my heart.
A self picture
I at a time of pleasure
Describes this feeling
Of my life a lovely part.
Not vainness not praise
Not being a beauty
It is an inner self
My thoughts portray.
Magic of a poet's dream
Life that goes on each day.
Any happening feeling or scenes
A poet's playground
Through their eyes to see.
People all surrounding
As a poem in my thoughts
Become a part of me.
So my picture a poet
My face a mirror of my mind
An out loves
An inner love
To poets everywhere
I am one of you
Poetry last over years
Over time.

Victoria Joan Theedam

Catherine

I love my love and she loves me true,
She cheers me up when I am blue.
She looks so lovely dressed in red,
As she gently tosses back her head.
She looks a dream in black and white
I just can't get her out of sight.
When we dance I hug her tight
She floats on air just like a kite.
I can't help but kiss her lips -
It sends me on a thousand trips.
Yes, of her I am very fond,
My love and I have a special bond.
For me, there will be no other,
Than my darling, Catherine, my lover.

Paul Malcolm Kimber

Countersigned

(For: Seamus Heanney whose 'Postscript' I acknowledge)

Yes, Seamus, I can vouch the Flaggy Shore,
When we made time to drive to County Clare
And at our ease surveyed the limestone slabs,
Tide-polished, eon-impressed coral stems
As delicate a marbling over wrought,
But vivid gentians captivate the eye
Couching amid the gryke-bound tufts of thrift.
Then walking from the lonely, sombre lake
We're overtaken by the rain, wind-swept
Into a sudden elemental broil
Against a tide that, surging past New Quay,
Frustrates a heron spearing for its meal,
And drives us to the warmth of Linnane's Bar.
We late return beneath a crescent moon
As Black Head looms mysterious through the mist.
I hear a hooting solitary owl
Accompany the voice of wind and sea.

Jim Finch

Tour Eiffel

Tall and slender,
A mighty tower of steel,
Hovering gracefully over the
Parisian skyline,
A gracious work of art.

And all around you,
The romantic secrets of a city unfold,
Clothed in ethereal beauty
And fairy-tale charm.

Like moths to a light
Your admirers flock,
Overwhelmed and enchanted
By the magnetic power of your presence.

But there are those who fail to notice you,
As they go about their everyday tasks,
Lost in a world of their own,
A world where your magic fails to have effect.

Yet, a landmark you are
And always will be
In a place where everything seems possible
And the dreams of starry-eyed lovers come true.

N Yogaratnam

Safe In The Arms Of Jesus

Two baby boys to heaven are gone
One named David the other John
To me they brought so much pleasure
Each of them a little treasure.
They weren't able to run about
To mischief make or scream and shout.
With special aids and TLC
They lived their lives as well as could be.
Their innocent smiles, I couldn't resist,
I can picture them now - how they are missed.
But I'll see them some day beyond the skies
And then there'll be no more goodbyes.
So, safe in the arms of Jesus they rest
Because in the end, God knows what's best.

Anne Black

My Girl

This is my daughter Charmaine
Always acting the clown
Forever a smile on her face
Hardly ever a frown
She was a lot younger then
So cute and so good
To have kept her like that?
If only I could
She is sixteen now
Sometimes naughty and bad
But I still stand by her
Because I am her dad
And I'll always love her
Because she's still my little girl
It will be that way forever
I know that it will

Eric Dunn-Fox from Leek

Lady

(Written for my boyfriend because of his love and dedication
to his Cavalier King Charles.)

She's a girl so lovely,
One whose got it all,
A wonderful personality,
Features dainty and small.
Beautiful long dark hair,
Ebony eyes that sparkle and shine,
Heart so full of love,
Intelligent and refine.
Her loyalty's unconditional,
Beauty to turn any man's head,
Greets me with a kiss each evening,
Lying regally on my bed.
Who is this goddess?
I hold so dear,
Is she my wife, my lover?
No, she's my Cavalier . . .

Sandra Austin

The Timeless Land

Land of a thousand dreams, islands of a million charms:
Cassiterides, land of the blest,
Archipelago of Paradise, amidst the azure sea.
Mother to her people and graveyard to the mariner,
Haunted by ghosts of a lost time:
Spirits of centuries before,
Their silent cries reach out through the pale eyes of wooden figureheads,
Scotsman, Queen of Spain, Eagle, Devon Maid,
Once proud and varnished on a gallant helm,
Now weather-beaten and barnacled - lying on an island shore.
Bryher Samson, Tresco, St Mary's,
All gentle harbours in the summer's sun lapped by billowing wavelets
Until the winter fury of the mad Atlantic gales,
Remnants of a past gazing down upon the present:
The still unchanging sea which respects neither Time nor Man
On this timeless land of Scilly.

Roberta Gray

Emancipation

Emerging from shadow, reluctant, unaware
That hopes may lie ahead. Should she dare
Venture yet further?
Draped, clothed, wrapped with shame
Of knowing she is woman - unconsidered . . .

Now blushing with exposure, she reveals
Her willingness to offer, feed and heal
A world half-hopeful for a partner's touch.
Close by hovers one white hope,
Abandoned to the glance of lechery.

Final emergence, sunlit - and yet half shade,
Triumphant statement - is it clearly made
When - somewhere - faintly in the window's face
Another face reflects its thoughts of worth?

Audrey M E Davies

Camera Shy!

I love my pet rabbits, I have seven in all,
They come in various sizes,
the short and fat, the thin and tall.

In many ways they're like humans,
as each one has ways that differ.
One's very frisky, one's nervous of plastic,
and another that's a real good sniffer!

They dig deep in the garden, and lay down their scents
And view neighbours' foundations, or base of a fence.
I rush for the camera, and dash back outside,
but by this time I've scared them,
and they've all gone to hide!

I crouch in a corner keeping silent and still
for *them* to emerge of their own free will.
The camera's all set, the sun is still bright,
If they don't come out soon I'll be here until night!

Their trust in me is so sure, food and love, they beg for more,
But when I am trying to get a 'good shot'
they make sure my plans just all 'go to pot'!
Confidence restored, they're out on the grass
and washing their paws . . .
because I've long given up hope - and gone back indoors!

Lynne Cotton

Ephesus

Night was spent in Selcuk town
High, modern houses, shops, souvenirs,
Muddy ponds from last night's rain,
Cafes, shops full of cheap trinkets, cards,
But now, just minutes along a winding road
I stand on ground, trod foot by foot
Through centuries of time and tide, this
Harbour town, now miles from sea
While tourists gape and wonder we.

Emperor Hadrian, Artemis, St Paul
Apostle, preacher saint, have all stood here and walked
The long road downhill to Celsus Library
Magnificent in years gone by and now,
Restored in part, so close your eyes,
Hear carriages, talk, tales, and lovers
From centuries gone by.

Within the theatre 24,000 sat listening,
Watching, smells of lions, fighting,
Actors orating, silversmiths shouting
As Paul tried, he only did his best
To tell Ephesians of Christ,
And now, eats empty, drains blocked, hospital destroyed,
Temple blocks in ruins, a scrap only to
Tell the stories of lives gone past.

Do we care more than did those men
To whom Paul spoke of Jesus' love?
I wondered, as German, French, Japanese, Greek,
and Turkish went about this day in 1997
Will we find our way to heaven?

Elizabeth M Sudder

Moving On

The years have flown and now I must look
Forward - never back.
The friends I've made along the way, their
Time I shall not lack.
A happy home it's always been, the times were good
Though sometimes lean.
The children now have flown the nest -
And I shall too - it's for the best.
My partner's gone to a greater place
So life for me's a slower pace.
But memories will never die.
New house awaits and yet I sigh.
I hope that soon it's home sweet home
And never more I'll need to roam.
I'll settle down and start again
And always shall remember when
We were two.

Sandra Capper

All Washed Up

Why do you keep sniggering
and peeping round the door?
It isn't that remarkable
we have done this before.

It wasn't Lucy's christening
it was ages after that,
You made us chips for tea and
burned your hand with red-hot fat.

You had to wear a bandage
which you hadn't to get wet
I washed dishes all that week,
Don't you remember pet?

What puzzles us is why you
ladies think it such a bind.
We find it quite refreshing
therapeutic to the mind.

Well you've had your bit of fun
so how's-about-a cuppa?
We will return the favour
when you wash-up after supper!

Lorna Green

The Tale Of A Kangaroo

'I've found a friend,' said the kangaroo
as it nibbled the sweet, fresh grass,
'My paddock is bare, there's none left in there
but along came this old Pommy lass,
She's gathered up armfuls from under the trees
and brought it in here for my mates and me
The word got around, so we're having a feast
We're all friends together now see!'

'Now isn't this nice,' I said to the big 'roo,
'I've watched your pals out in the bush
You've plenty of veg here, but you like sweet green grass
My grandson's brought some more - so don't push!'
What a grand time we had with those creatures
just showing kindness and doing no harm
I'll always remember that strange 'tea-party'
And a gentle 'roo's hand holding my arm.

Hannah M French

A Special Place

The flames have sunk, just like the moon,
There's only embers glowing;
And in our hearts we know that soon
Each of us must be going.

We've sung tonight and laughed tonight,
With friends both old and new.
There's some would say we're not quite right
But they haven't got a clue.
A campfire is a special place,
To share some time and thought,
You'll always find a friendly face
And fun that can't be bought.

We're all sung out, it's getting cold,
But our hearts will long be warmed,
By the tunes we've learnt and stories told
And the stunts we've seen performed.

As we wish each other safe and well,
Before finally retiring,
Let's hope there's only a short spell
'Til we're once again camp-firing!

P Sharratt

Mountain Stream

In the beginning, only a trickle
Silently flowing downstream
Gathering speed and getting stronger
Rushing over stones
Gushing down ravines
Into milky cascades
Running ever deeper and wider
Until it reaches a mass of icy cold water

Margaret Monaghan

Who Wants An Easy Life?

It isn't always easy
Looking after a boy of three
When you are no longer young
You haven't got the energy
To always keep up with him

The early mornings take their toll
I used to find it hard to sleep
But I've no insomnia now.
Some days I feel too tired to think

We go to the playgroup twice a week
That's something we both enjoy
We do the gardening some days
And go for walks when it's fine

You keep on going somehow
Wondering just how you do it.
But when you feel like giving up
A little hand takes yours
And looking up, with eyes of blue,
He says, 'Granny I love you,'
And you know it's all worthwhile.

Margaret C Rae

A Mariner's Delight

A church on the hill, tall steeple in the west
Sailing barges moored in the river estuary
Maldon in Essex, on the edge of Blackwater
Its charming appeal that never falters

A stroll along the promenade, pretty scenic views
Where house-boats and small boats by the quay they cruise
The Jolly Sailor inn, a timeless smugglers' den
Of copper pots and toby jugs, yarns and merry men
Bygone days of wooden ships and glowing lantern lights
Quaint and picturesque, as the red sky at night.

Rita Humphrey

Horton Tower

Alone it stands on Horton Hill
This lofty ruin six storeys high
By Jeffrey Archer designed with a quill
As a game observatory in days gone by

A famous architect's creation
Steeped in its own history
Some say it was a smugglers' station
Now an empty shell of mystery

It wore a cupola back in time
Of lead shaped like a dome
But that was then, when in its prime
Over two hundred years ago

When upward winding stairs did rise
And a fireplace carved from stone
Unglazed windows where huntsmen's eyes
Watched the wild deer that roamed

Then war took its toll of body and home
The depression brought hardship and pain
Hence the tower was stripped of its precious dome
Thus ending an era and reign

Lashed by gales its brickwork eased
Now a ruin, where rooks have nested
And in between them creeping ivy has squeezed
Tufts of grass grow where once the dome rested

Left crumbling on the skyline it towers
Whilst others decide its fate
Helpless and without any power
It patiently stands and waits

Now rescue plans are sought to repair
The folly with its turrets three
To stop decay and preserve with care
Our heritage for the next century.

Heather Bleach

Wee Maria

'A giggle a day keeps the Doctor away'
I do believe that's true
I know an outstanding example
Which I'll now tell to you.
Once I had a friend called Maria
Whom you can see in the photograph
Whenever you met her she was giggling
Always making people laugh.
She was so full of mischief
Her 'joie de vivre' was contagious
Far better than pill or potion
As her sense of humour was outrageous.
She believed in the Power of Prayer
And took life's troubles in her stride,
Gong by the Wee Happy Bus to visit a sick friend
On the day before she died.
People all called her 'Aunt Maria'
She was well known and loved by everyone,
As she never moaned or wallowed in self-pity
Even when life was no bundle of fun.
'Good Gear comes in small Packages'
She was only four foot eleven
She laughed and giggled until the age of ninety nine.
I'm sure that she's now causing havoc in Heaven.

Mary Anne Scott

Four Legged Friend

The greatest friend that man can have
Is the friend with four legs.
He will sit by your side when you are sad
Head on your lap his nose in your hand
Big dark eyes full of trust
For him a walk a day is a most
He does not ask for very much
A few scraps from your plate
And lots of love
He will not argue or disagree
But trust you implicitly
He will sit on your lap while you doze
And wake you up with a lick on your nose
He will let you know when strangers approach
He does not like thunder
And will cower under your chair
But is soon reassured when he knows you are there
While you have a dog you are never alone
You can talk to them and always be right
But still they won't let you out of their sight
Just remember as with a human
So it is with a dog
A friend is forever so treat them with love.

Joan Fowler

My Granddaughter Natasha

My granddaughter Natasha,
So happy and bright,
She loves the Spice Girls,
Dances to their music, most of the night,
She smiles at people on the bus,
They give her plenty of fuss,
Her face lights up
She's given some money,
I say! 'Keep smiling honey.'
She helps me in my home,
Chats away on the phone,
Telling people what she thinks
She'll grow up, strong and proud,
The boys will be giving her winks,
Barbie is her favourite doll
Bedroom is Barbie, wall to wall,
Large Barbie dolls, and some small,
She runs through my door,
With crisps and lolly,
She gives me a cuddle and kiss,
Saying 'I love you Nanny!'
I hope she visits me, when she's a housewife,
We'll be friends, the rest of my life.

Patricia Rogers

Warning

Before you decide to take me home,
This warning I must impart.
I'll dig up your garden,
Chew up your house,
    - And worse -
I'll steal your heart.

Karen Hunton

Life Was Wonderful Then

Lovely the memories
Of when you were young
The sweet happy days
Of adventure and fun
As we learned together
To share and to love
How quickly the years
Seem to fly as they must
Your growing up years
They came and they went
But I was so happy
My life was content
And now you are grown up
I look back to when
You were small, good the days
Life was wonderful then

Jeanette Gaffney

Kissing Barn

Ewe dog together said
Sheep snog Jack Russell bred
My biscuits you dared pick
So! Accept amorously a lick.

We terriers know not fear
Your cheek display my dear
Gender female both we
No sexual connotations see.

From farm dogs, be chaste
Working sheep I think waste
Rats and cats supply exercise
For sheep, you have delicious eyes.

Sheer woolly thinking divides span
Platonic friendship's ram and man
Spilt food can agree share
I bark seductively, you responsively baa baa.

Those in house call me Peg
What they you! Is that bloody pet teg
Sheepwise better thief than Siamese Cat
Compulsively, must kiss you again on that.

In China some eat dogs
Limbs in France disappear off frogs
Even pet lambs into freezer leg
On this farm, best learn to beg.

Please! In name of mutton another kiss
One deviant in flock won't amiss
Nice and secluded in barn
How can camera do any harm?

Alf Jones

Unfair

Up you creak singing sweetly
Turning with the steel frame
Just hanging like someone hanging
Spitting below without aim

Then the man releases the brake
You see - life is hideously cruel
We are only happy for a while
Before reality and routine both call

It's all a broken down fun fair
With pleasure rides numbering one
C'est la vie, mon amie. C'est la vie
We live until all hope is gone

Damian Ward

The Metallic Bird

Silver up above and looking very small
Speeding along with no effort at all
Its heavy load it handles with ease
And commands respect from all it sees

It travels so high over land, sea and city
Powerful, ambitious with an air of dignity
Surveying the cold lands and hot lands too
Enjoying its great panoramic view

At the end of each journey it joins our terrain
To the welcome of sunshine, snowstorm or rain
It stands there so regal and towering high
It's so impressive when down from the sky

What is this object so powerful and strong
So gracious though tall and extremely long
It is the spectacle built by man
To fly in the sky as fast as it can
Our aeroplanes and since then our jets
Flash in the sky as the sun sets

Maureen Stewart-Condron

Your Shoes

Seeing your shoes on the floor
Standing side by side
Empty now they'll always be
Our paths had to divide
When I think of all the places
Where your shoes have tread
And I was always with you
My hand you held and led.

But standing now on the floor
Those shoes won't walk any more
I'll leave them there side by side
And when I look
I feel such pride
Your shoes mean so much to me
For when we walked
We felt free
I'll leave them there
Side by side
Our paths in life
Did not divide.

Marjorie Ann Warden

Tribute To A Headmaster

There's a new headmaster at the school
He has brown hair and is quite tall
Large blue kindly eyes
Behind round glasses hide

A good sense of humour, on the arrogant side
A friendly grin that he never hides
Treats children with respect, rarely shouts
Of illness and self pity he has bouts

Family man, a dapper dresser
Looks harassed when under pressure
Shouldn't work Sundays, often looks tired
A good night's sleep is what's desired

Wine connoisseur, Manchester United fan
A caring, sensitive, gentle man
Sarcastic in a playful way
Looks pale by the end of day

Manager, politician, not afraid of hard work
Sorting out the problems that in schools lurk
As a headmaster he's with the best
And would be missed if he left.

Agnes Jones

Perfection

My Father's Mother.
Big and stout, all of eighteen stone.
Broad as tall.

Feather filled pillow breasts.
Custom made to embrace.
Out in front like a ship set full sail.

Ever shrouded in grieving black.
Legs encased in concertina wool hose.
Feet in bunion stretched colour beyond recall carpet slippers.

Candyfloss grey hair, pink pate peeking through.
Dragged tight back dearth of hair bun at nape of neck.
Crinkled white tissue paper skin, blue vein decorated.
Brown age spot speckled.

Perfection.
With all the time and love in the world for me.

Patricia Scott

Captive

up, down and around

The hulking tiger paces
the perimeter of its prison

up, down and around

Long fluid strides on pads
the size of a man's palm
have worn the path to smooth marble

up, down and around
the hulking tiger paces

Once bright eyes have dulled,
and dreams of freedom
shimmer like so much gold dust
just out of reach

up, down and around
the hulking tiger paces

up, down and around

C S Robinson

Innocence Of A Child

Innocence of a child,
Wrapped up for winter,
The smile of happiness about him,
The future still before him.

The joy of what is before him,
Not certain in this world,
But still with a heart of innocence,
The picture so it tells.

Mary Jo West

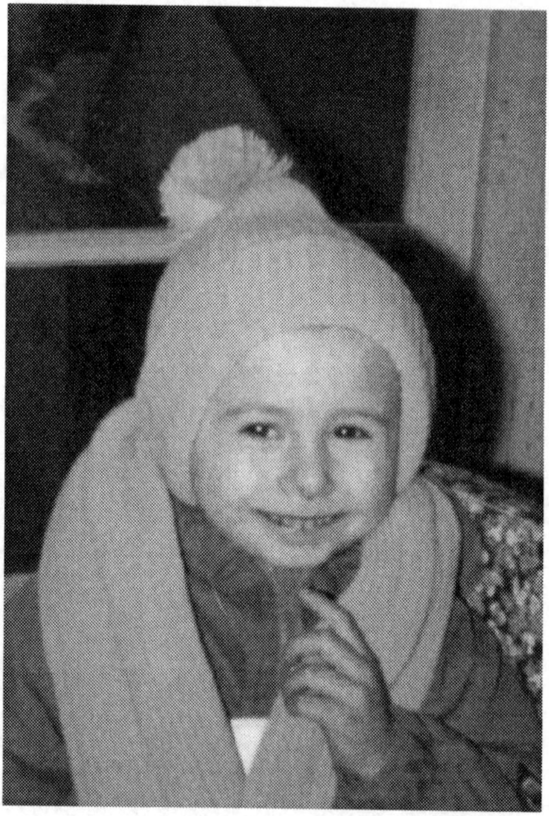

Linda Swings

Busy the swing in describing its arc,
bends low the branch of my old apple-tree -
safely-tied ropes, while abrading the bark,
creak with complaint at the load - six stone three.

Halted the swing for a youth-age exchange,
placid three-score to his digging gives pause -
flowers of fancy, a nine-year old's range,
proffer a 'Why' and demand a 'Because.'

Dainty and dappled with tree-filtered light,
auburn-haired Linda is working like steam -
loving each moment of to and fro flight,
prettier pendulum never was seen.

T C Hudson

Precious Moments

Twelve o'clock was our precious moments together
We talked, we laughed and cried
Of family and friends, and stories untold
We talked of things unimportant to some
And held onto ourselves with pride
Mum was so lonely after dad had died
Hardly a moment passed when she hadn't cried
The distance between us wasn't easy to cover
But twelve o'clock the phone would ring
And happiness to both would bring
As we told our stories, belief and concern
One year and a half this went on in return
Until the Lord decided to take mum on his side
He had watched in concern as she utterly cried
Together with his blessings she met up with dad
And now she is happy with God up above
God bless you both.

Your daughter

Glenys M Bowell

On Leaving Caldey Island

We sat and waited on the shore,
As little boats went back and fore,
'Til fading light, and setting sun,
Denoted that the day was done;
With heavy hearts, and feet of clay,
Across the sand we made our way;
With each impression of our track,
We knew, we never would go back . . .

Dorothy Neil

Douglas, Lanarkshire

In the valley, our village stands proudly
able to hold its head high.
Steeped in history old buildings, in ruins,
remain in honour of days gone by.

Local historians take pleasure recounting
tales of battles of yesteryear:
how the good Sir James Douglas fought valiantly
bravely displaying no fear.

Touring the area by foot is rewarding:
scenic walks abound.
Take in the sites as you amble:
history, and wildlife too, is all around.

We've made history again with a windfarm:
the first of its kind in this land.
We look to the future while remembering the past
this is Douglas, near Lanark, Scotland.

Helen Crawford

The First Fall Of Winter's Snow

How singularly beautiful is the first fall of winter's snow
When draped pristinely over frosty bough
Carved lace beguiling naked branch
Sparkling and dazzling in the winter light.
The many different shapes of tree revealed
Like persons dressed for some fantastic ball
Glistening and shining in the softest mist
Of tiny pearlised flakes of diamante sequins
Turning and shimmering in the breathy air.
What magic mystery can we see
In the first fall of the winter's snow?

The Painter in Words

A Helping Hand

The good Lord above
Sends out his love
For all mankind to share
Everybody is in His care
No matter what people do or say
He still loves us in a great way
In times of trouble he helps us along
To show us the right from the wrong
Our lifespan is so very brief
He helps us overcome our grief
And when we are happy he is too
He makes the sun shine in a sky of blue
When it rains and tears come down
He puts a rainbow in the sky all around
The good Lord above
Sends out his love

Ann Sylvia Franks

Little Flower Girl

One fine day in May, I walked,
And to a little girl I talked,
She sat there, making flower-chains,
Her fingers dyed, with flowery stains,
I said to her, 'That's very good,'
She then looked up, to where I stood,
'Thank you Sir, it's for a friend,
And if she's good, I'll let her lend,'
'It's very pretty, I'm sure she'll like,'
'I do hope so, I like her bike,'
I said goodbye, and began to think,
Of my conversation, with the girl in pink,
Today my walk, had been worthwhile,
This 'Little Flower Girl' had made me smile.

Christopher A J Evans

My Girl

Early one sunny October morn
My Bonnie baby girl was born
With gray-green eyes and cheeks of rose,
Just like a flower as she grows,
A Friday's child is loving and giving
And makes many lives
Well worth the living.
My girl now is kind and caring.
Always thoughtful, always sharing.
Sometimes she will ride life's merry-go-round
And once in a while her feet leave the ground,
But her love can't be taken for granted
Or to your cost you soon will find
She can be quite the opposite
Of caring and kind,
My girl now is a woman grown
And has an equanimity
All her very own.

Constance J Roper

Herald Of Free Enterprise

I speak of the ferry of disaster
Which left the port of Zebrugge
March '87 was the year
And the fatalities were huge

It was down to a human error
Someone forgot to close the door
Half a mile out, the hull was full
And the Enterprise tipped o'er

Focusing his thoughts on the terrifying events of just 48 hours before, William Cardwell nestles back in a sofa at his home in [illegible] — with total recall — describes the horror and the heroism of the 10 minutes after the "Herald" ferry capsized.

Darkness fell as the lights went out
Everyone screaming and thrashing about
Grabbing and pulling each other down
Praying 'Dear God don't let me drown'

A few of them there, kept their heads
Otherwise many more would be dead
Saving lives with little thought of their own
Just wishing everyone could return home

I recall this night, though I was not there
I was safe at home in my armchair
A terrible tragedy, I wish for no other
And I thank the Lord daily for the return of my brother.

Joan Halliday

Holiday Snaps

After the Castle Museum we had a look around
Weary of feet, Mum and I sat down
But for the wicked there being no rest
And at my friend Julie's behest
We had to pose and smile for her snap
Usual holiday photos, we ended up looking like prats
Just to give us memories of our trip up north
To the walled and many museumed city of York

Melanie M Burgess

Skeleton Jake

Hi there folks yes it's me
A skeleton I thought I'd be
I like to dress up when I can
Behind all this I have a plan,
Into the kitchen I must go
Quietly, carefully on tiptoe,
I think I'll get something nice to eat
This will be a special treat,
Quickly now or I'll get caught
Not to touch I'm always taught
So don't tell anyone what you've seen
They'll only think that you've had a dream,
But just in case there's some mistake
I'm not a skeleton I'm really Jake.

Chris Gardner

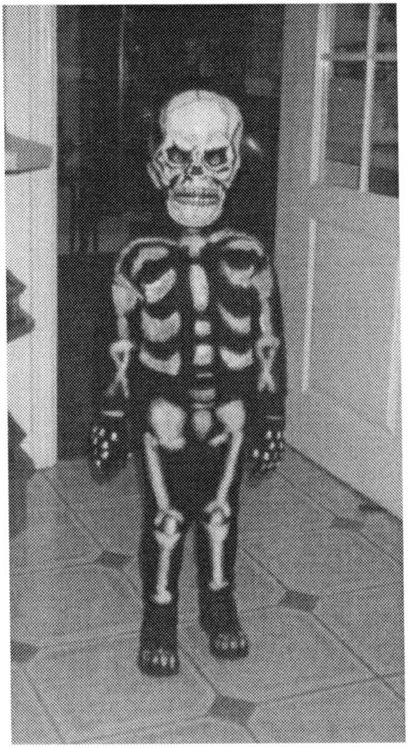

The Iron Man

(Statue In Birmingham)

There is a new statue in Birmingham,
It's rusty, and leans like the Tower of Pizza,
It's called 'The Iron Man'
It sure was a laugh when I leaned on it,
While my friend took a photograph.

It's unusual to say the least,
But, it's funny, and quite cute to me,
I just want to keep going to see it,
This rusty statue in Birmingham,
It's kind of friendly, 'The Iron Man'

What did the sculptor have in mind?
Did he mean to make it lean?
It really is, the funniest statue,
That I have ever seen.
It has no arms, no hands, no face!
Although it leans to one side,
Somehow it has an air of grace.

It's supposed to represent, 'The Iron Industry'
Of days of factories of steel and toil,
Men working hard, hot, and full of sweat,
An industry Birmingham will not forget,
For 'The Iron Man' statue will remind folk,
That life was hard, for the men in steel,
Life for them was no joke.

Ruth Dunstan

Smile, Smile, Smile

My friend Margaret and me
are sitting on our float
in the carnival,
Which is a coal lorry,
made into a bed,
We are trying to look
and pose like real models!
Wearing baby-doll nighties
and showing a lot of leg
(That's me sitting on the edge)
Permanent smiles on our face
On our feet we have fluffy slippers
Our props - are umbrellas trimmed with lace.
Crowds of people with cameras
All shouting 'Look this way,'
Margaret had to keep making me laugh
Smile, smile, smile,
is what we did all day
Had to look happy for the photographs.
Through smiling so much
our faces were sore
Us be professional models!
No way -
It would be such a bore,
Having to smile at the camera
Every day.

Linda Roberts

Babies

Babies are bonny and beautiful
babies are innocent too.
Some have eyes of brown,
others have eyes of blue.

They're helpless and so trusting
with skin so soft and sweet.
Their tiny hands are lovely
and so are their tiny feet.

If you love and pet them
they'll gurgle and they'll coo.
The love they show you in return
means all the world to you

Babies are delightful
to neglect them is a crime.
Shelter and protect them,
and give them a little time.

Vera Seddon

Thanks!

We really were delighted when our prizes came along,
Especially as we all enjoy to entertain with song.
We love to sing for fun and give a lot of people pleasure
But a prize from Gilwell Park is truly something we can treasure

So if you ever need the 27th Walthamstow
To entertain in any way, we'd love to 'Have-a-go.'
We have a repertoire of songs that's really quite extensive,
Which will delight and please and will in no way be offensive.

We've sung at concerts, weddings too, and much to our surprise
At Phillips' National Tape Contest we won a special prize.
And now we're off to choose our books with pride and happiness
From Victor, Peter, Joseph, Keith, we say goodbye, God Bless!

Norah G Carter

The English Telephone Box

I adore the English telephone box,
The K6 is my favourite style.
With its architectural structure,
You can see it from a mile!

I adore the English telephone box,
It's painted in a delightful red.
It's part of our English heritage,
Its disappearance is something I dread!

I adore the English telephone box,
One day I'd like one of my own.
I'll keep it clean and well painted,
In my garden will be its home!

Janis N Betteridge

Lara's Academy Of Dance

Every Wednesday evening
to dancing class we go
first we limber up
then it's heel to toe

We practise our tap steps
with all of our might
then we practise the steps again
until we get them right

So after our tap lesson
we all need a drink
then we practise our ballet steps
it's much harder than you think

We hold on to the bars
dream of becoming ballet stars
stretch our legs to make them strong
sometimes we get the positions wrong

You may think we sound like elephants
rehearsing the Sugar Plum Fairy dance
but I believe one day you will see
what talented dancers we all have turned out to be.

V Stott

My Little Mate

My little brother Jamie
he thinks he's got it all
He thinks he's got great muscles
but he's just skinny and tall
But I have to go along with him
and say, yes you look just great
Because after all he's only 10
and he's my little mate

Charmaine Dunn-Fox from Leek

A Day At The Farm

Come on Grandad let's go to the cows
Come on Grandad let's go to the goats
Come on Grandad before it's too late
Oh Grandad the keeper decided to close the gates
Oh never mind we will have to come back at a later date.

M Whittle

Polar The Bear

He looks at me, but never moves
He is quiet and behaves himself -
With eyes so bright, and coat so soft.
He is a mascot, and a cuddly toy.

If I speak to him, he seems to know -
That I really love him so,
He sits upon my knee -
A real true friend he will always be.

When I clean the house, he's thrown about -
But when work is done to a T,
He relaxes on the divan with me.
He loves his favourite pillow,
The one that's red and yellow.

He is cheap to keep,
He doesn't eat.
No need to buy him fish or meat.
It would be too much for me to *bear*.

If he really was not there
Would never, ever be the same
And Polar is his name.

M E Smith

Washday Capers

Joss and Kiri like to play,
Run jump and hide away.
Peek-a-boo is lots of fun,
Can be played by anyone.

The laundry basket empty,
Makes a super toy.
No peeping, count to ten,
You go first, it's my turn then.

In the basket Kiri goes,
Hides right under Joss's nose!

Jessica Fraser

My Grandad

My Grandad, a pipe he always did smoke,
Everyone thought it quite a joke
when I got one too!
Of course it was new,
He took me for a walk every day
and we smoked together along the way,
Friends and strangers used to laugh and stare
but I didn't care,
My Grandad made smoke come out
I couldn't do that, but I did cut my teeth
on it, without any doubt.

Edna Parrington

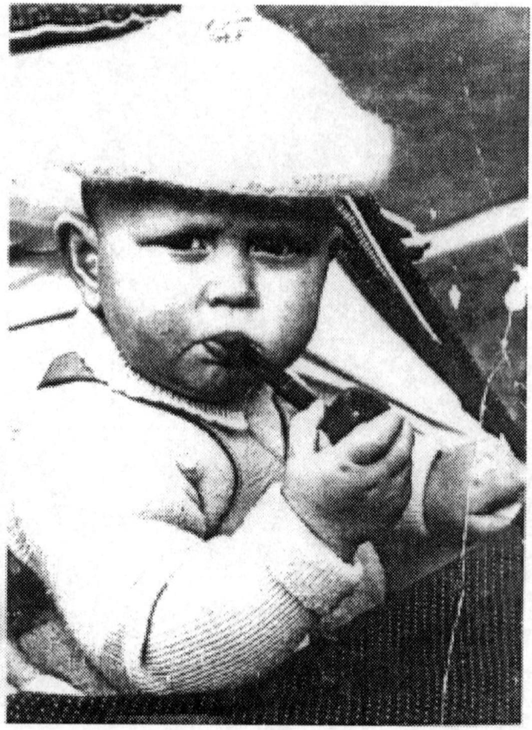

A Morning Stroll

Good Morning Mr Badger
Are you going for a stroll
Yes, just around the garden
Are you coming Mr Mole

I'd be delighted Badger
If I can hold on tight
I know my way beneath the ground
But have trouble in sunlight

Hold tight then, said the Badger
And whilst we take a stroll
I'll introduce you to the new folk
Would you like that Mr Mole?

Meet Snow White and the seven dwarfs
And now meet Bill and Ben
They live in two big flower-pots
Nice to see them once again

Here's Pedro, the new Donkey
With his saddle-basket flowers
He's made a lot of fuss of
As he stands around for hours

Oh dear! Here's the dog back
We'd best beat a retreat
But I'll paw the ground to tell you
When there's more new folk to meet.

Bell Ferris

Dreamland

If you've ever been to Dreamland
You will know just what I mean.
For it is something that is part of you,
Something you have seen.
Mine, is an island with a lighthouse
Stretched out in the sea,
Which brings precious memories
Flooding back to me.
The smell of the sea
And the mist in the air
I only have to picture it
And I feel as though I'm there.
Only for a second
Did I feel that inner glow
But something seemed to tell me,
And I couldn't let it go.
Slowly, as we sailed away
Towards our destination,
I knew that I had captured
My piece of inspiration.

Barbara Hellewell

Round Barrows In A Rapefield

Two myrtle mounds crouch catlike
in a sudden sea of chrome
guarding sacred land
where iron bones fashioned from ochre burnt
are returned to ancestral loam
the citrus acre sings out
unashamed as a suburban parlour in the midday sun

yellow is our rape of the earth
and Vincent's last blazing look at a cornfield world
against black, fleeing crows
over the Mendip horizon a viridian fringe of trees
swish like a crematorium backdrop

only a week later, cut down by the lammas scythe
my mother's dead jaw hangs slack
in a green/yellow field of a face
far from where the Russian steppes of her birthland
billow with golden wheat

now, olev ha shalom (may they rest in peace),
both parents lie scattered husks on foreign soil
while its original occupants are exiled under margarine
yitgadahl v'yitkadash shmey rabah
for all our ancestors
sing unashamedly yellow in the midday sun!

Rachael Clyne

Beetle Catchin'...

I'm a beetle catchin' feline, that's my forte,
a catcher of all beetles large and small,
I catch flies and I catch spiders, I catch woodlice,
but the silverfish I like the best of all.

I've learnt (much to my cost), not to tangle with a wasp,
nor a lazy droning humble bumble bee,
But it's all to no avail, the sting is in the tail,
as I found out the day that one stung me.

I had a brief encounter with an earwig,
which hung upon my lip and made me wince
I didn't know the power of their pincers,
I do now . . . so avoid them ever since.

I wait so patiently for daddy longlegs,
to make his slow descent down to the ground,
No sooner has his feet touched on the carpet,
I'm over, in one mighty leaping bound.

If I am sleeping soundly on my cushion,
and mother mentions 'Moff' . . . I'm wide awake,
Like a spring I'm tightly wound,
I'm there without a sound, but sometimes (I confess) I am too late.

There's this pesky fly called a blue-bottle,
the nastiest of flies I've ever seen,
It really is quite rude . . . they 'do things' on our food,
(I still maintain its colour is more green.)

Mother has a laugh when I jump into the bath,
and at the sloping end there is this giant,
I advance and he'll retreat, on all of his eight feet,
I find he can be really must defiant.

He cannot make the slope, so I sit and wait and hope,
sure enough my patience is rewarded,
He comes sliding back again, shoots past me to the drain,
and in the bung-hole I find he's resided.

I sat and watched an armour-plated woodlouse,
as it wandered aimlessly across the hall,
But when I tried to pat it with my soft paw,
the bloomin' thing rolled up into a ball.

I never get fed-up, tho' I'm a house cat,
there's always something here to catch my eye
I shall leave now, and I hope you will excuse that,
I must investigate that butterfly . . .

Joyce G Tryhorn

Remembering

(Maggie Wall)

A monument of stone
Complete with cross
Perchance belied
The haunting - of
A Scottish moor
Where Maggie's
'Witches thimbles'
Spired

Emotive thoughts
Engaged my conscience
As mountain thyme
I pressed within
A sprig
Of heath bell heather
By a sullied
Tarnished pin.

Irene Gunnion

The Seagull

To harbour stack his curved claws cling,
In anticipation poised each wing,
As back to port the catch they bring.

Across the bar the fleet arrives,
Glint of sun on gutting knives.
Down with raucous cry he dives.

Geraldine Page

A Poem?

Aye, anywei, ah wuz thinkin' o' writin' this poem
Jist aboot whit's gawn thru' ma heid, y'know, jist
Thoats an' that, pittin' thum doon oan papurr.
Evun goat a pen ready in aw, dead prufeshunnul like.

But, it's funny, 'cause it's no as if it's anythin'
Important, jist aw soarts o' ideas an that, y'know
An it seems weeird, sayin' it's poetry like, 'cause
It's jist rubbish really, the wei yi think aboot things.

So, anywei, ah wuz gonny write it aw doon, intae wee
Verses an' that, no rhymin' stuff or nuthin', 'cause
Aw that seems soarta iffy, y'know, tears 'n fears an
Skies above an' love, ach, y'know whit a mean, eh?

Right, so ah wuz aw ready tae pit it doon, jist write
It as it comes, y'know, but ah felt a bit daft, y'know
'cause thurr wuz nane o' thae metaffurs an' similies.
Y'know, these weird names, litotes, like wee feet, eh?

An when ah thoat aboot it, a mean, how wid it look
Oan the papurr, ah thoat, whut'l peepul think, eh?
'cause yi think o' poets like Rabbie Burns an' that
Or they metaffisikul guys, Keats, an' Shelley an' at.

Ah know thut the day thur's loads o' uthurr guys an
Some o' their stuffs awright, y'know, that dub stuff
Or even that old guy, Betjumin . . . he wuz awright, eh?
Ah evun fun some o' his stuff funny, in a wei, y'know.

Anywei, thurr wuz aw this uthurr stuff tae, metres an
That, anapaestic or sumthin', an iambic feet, Christ
Eh! . . . Ah'd see ah doacturr if a hud them, widn't you?
So a thoat, it widnae be right, an a didnae bothurr.

Alex N Hay

Happy Families

(For Samantha and Darren)

'I hate you!'
'You big fat cow!'
'Stop it you two - *stop it now!*'

'Who needs a sister?'
'Who wants a brother?'
Heard all the insults, this wise old mother.

Insults that hurt me more than them,
Such strong emotions
From one 13, one 11.

'Mum, she kicked me'
'Dad, he pinched'
Hair being pulled, fists are clenched.

'He gets his own way'
'You always believe her'
Act as go-between, favouring neither.

Very brief moments they get on well,
Won't ever admit it. I can tell.

'I love you'
'I'm glad we're related'
Not heard often, that's understated.

Growing up though will come to rely
On one another
If, they try!

Susan Merrifield

Reflections

I've left something on life's window pane,
A fragment of hope to carefully collect
Before it's washed away with the condensation of life
Its droplets of perfect form
Reflecting the dreams of anonymous desires.
Yet through these small deposits of light
Are forms, carved out of heaven and hell
Draped with fashioned silk
And covered with pearls of stone dew,
A triumphant miscellany of colour bent sideways
Dotted with crooked branches persistently growing forward,
While frail tender voices whisper
Mourned photographic details of the lost child.
But through this embodiment of light I wonder
Was it a bead of condensation,
Or a tear perilously clinging to my eye
Afraid to drop?

Sally Colgate

Ben And Jamie In The Snow

What happened to the world we know
While we two slept last night?
Some magic fingers were at work
To turn it all pure white.

We've never seen the snow before,
Don't quite know what to do,
We put on hats and woollen gloves
And rubber wellies too.

Yesterday the grass was green
When we came out to play,
White blankets cover trees and shrubs
And everything today.

We've borrowed Mummy's bucket
And filled it up with snow,
We'll pile it up and pat it down
And watch our snowman grow.

We're just a bit bewildered,
We really did not know
That little people have such fun
While playing in the snow.

Margaret Curzon-Howe

The Old Churchyard

Ivy covered stones that once stood tall
Lie under leaves or by moss covered walls
Time stands still in this silent place
Grass has grown in every space
Names washed clean by winter rains
Never to be seen again
Distant voices far away
Trees bow down their heads and pray
Another age has passed us by
Now is the time to say goodbye
Somewhere a voice calls out my name
Forget me not
Come back again

Delyse Healey-Proctor

Brolly In The Snow

With the
first
fragile
flake's
feathery
fall

Nature steels herself for harsher climes.
This season, white's the only shade to wear
(And even brutish Sound's well muffled).
While crabbèd skies, of gloomy, grudging grey
Glower at the joyful scenes below.

And should I leave the snow for others' fun?
And should I, feeling old, recoil from life?
And should I . . . ?

Splat!

A snowball hits me, mid-soliloquy.
Recoil? Give up? Life's calling for me ***now*** . . .

To send a snowball down some hapless neck,
To polish up the runners of my sledge,
(Yee haa?)
To wear the very loudest of my gloves
And take
My brolly in the snow.

David Walker

Bathtime

Hey please don't take my photo
It makes me feel quite daft
Can't a chap have privacy
While he's sitting in his bath

I hang on to the bath sides
I'm not feeling very sure
And my mum's arm is round me
She makes me feel secure

I've made a lot of splashes
I even soaked my mum
Played a while with boat and duck
My bathtime's been quite fun

G Morrisey

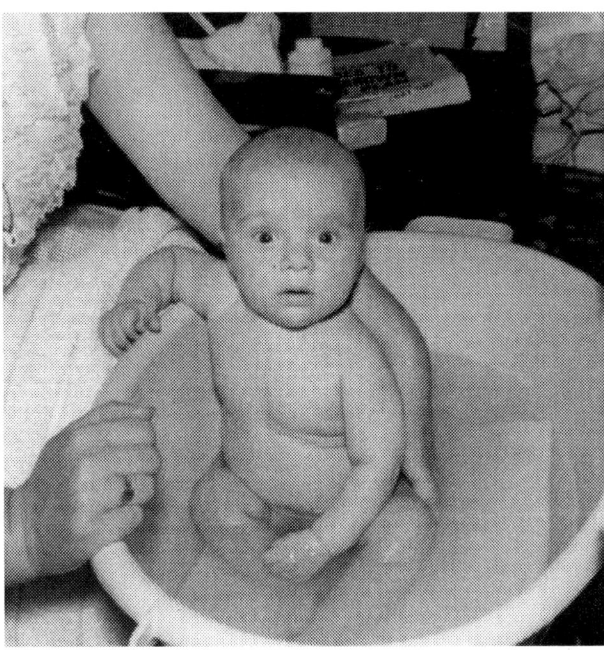

Our Haven

When friends come to visit
They always seem to say
How lovely the garden is
This compliment they pay.

The pink clematis now in bloom
Magnolia petals drop,
A blaze of colour all around
Another bud there to pop.

Wild birds find it a haven
Perhaps, no different from the rest,
With food and water a plenty
It may be to them, the best.

Seagulls soar overhead
So free in flight they go,
Peace and harmony found in the sky
No fear of any foe.

Our garden is our haven
Tranquillity we find
However rustic it may be
To us, no other kind.

Joyce White

The Lonely Little Bridesmaid

When mummy said I was to be a bridesmaid
I wasn't sure just what I'd have to do,
I knew that aunty Jane was getting married
And there would be a lovely party too.

The dress that Grandma made me was so pretty
'Twas shiny pink and reached down to my feet,
With flowers in my hair and in a basket
No wonder everybody said how sweet!

But in the church I suddenly felt lonely
'Cos mummy wasn't standing by my side
And though I tried so hard to be a good girl
I lost my nerve and just broke down and cried.

Then once more we were outside in the sunshine
My tears were dried and it was plain to see
The way folks smiled at me I'd been forgiven
Why bless her heart one said - she's only three.

Hazel Russell

Essence

Blooms of every size and colour,
Foliage to enhance their beauty,
Magnets to nature's feeders.

The serenity on a summer's eve,
Assorted aromas teasing the nose,
the blackbirds' twilight melody.

The raucous early choir
waking us from slumber,
Sunlight bathing the flora.

Each single petal sighing
welcoming the warming rays,
Bees queuing up for pollen.

Butterflies alighting on Buddleah,
Ants marching, worms excavating,
Birds pilfering the fruit trees.

Nature complementing man's labour,
Sounds and sights to enthral,
Encompassing the essence of the garden.

Glennis Horne

Camouflage

Not your usual type 'hols' like 'seen this' and 'done that'
more a case of 'some have eyes but do not see' that!
At first glance there seemed miles of savannah and stream
till the guide pointed out and we saw things for real.

We've seen huge rounded rocks nipping tufts off the trees
that have great flapping ears and blow trumpets to breathe,
And some gnarled knotted logs where the wild waters leap
that have sharp pointed teeth which they snap at great speed.

We've seen mud islands moving and yawning gaped mouths
that will snort at each other to warn as we pass
And some tightly close saplings through filtering light
which will gallop as one if they take sudden fright.

We've seen strange patterned creepers curled up into loops
that unspiral from branches and hiss as they swoop
But we never saw violence or slaughtered remains
nor the zoo-like discordance the 'tellies' all claim.

Just a primeval peace as the species all roamed
free to wade and to graze where the Zambezi flowed
While the only intrusions disrupting the scene
were our camera clicks and the jerks of a wheel.

Rosemary Keith

The River Bush

A little stream upon Mount Orra
It trickles down the hill
And flows o'er many a hill and dale
It may be in flood tomorrow.

Through Armoy village - past the mill
It slowly meanders on
Under the bridge and over the fall
The flow flows on and on.

The salmon leap and the trout sneak
Among the deep brown waters
A large grey heron flies above
The otters in the water.

Down through the emerald fields it flows
Under the pine tree standing bold
The sun gleaming upon a stone
The green algae floating alone.

Past the distillery it flows on and on.
Its journey is near an end.
Into the sea it hurries with pride
At Bushfoot it's away with the tide.

Elizabeth Jones

Sweet Dreams

Oh Santa I'm so lucky, to be sitting on your knee,
You hold me just like daddy, when he cuddles me,
I went to bed real early, because it's Christmas eve,
But suddenly I saw you: you were about to leave.

Oh Santa you are lovely, just how I thought you'd be,
So very kind and gentle, the same as daddy is to me,
My mummy she is also kind, she tucks me up each night,
kisses me and says 'God bless,' then puts out my light.

Oh Santa how I love you, your beard is soft and warm,
Just like my little pillow, it makes me want to yawn,
Tomorrow I will see my toys, knowing you have been,
But Santa I won't tell a soul; they'd say it was a dream.

Wenn The Penn

Hope

Come in and rest awhile.
Take time to meditate
On all the lovely things in life
And even as you wait

The birds will sing for you.
Behind will be the rain.
The sun will shine in Heaven's blue
And hope will spring again.

And as the old church walls
Surround you as you pray
God's blessings will encircle you
As you step out each day.

Joyce M Turner

My Last Duchess

That's my last Duchess from an aged album
Looking as if she were alive. I call
That piece a wonder, now: a human hand
Worked busily for a moment, and there she sits.
Alive. Will't please you sit and look at her?
The depth and passion of her earnest glance,
Tells all. It was her husband's presence
That forced her to be seated while he,
Victorian to the core and Man of God,
Stands diminished by God's delphiniums.
She had a heart - too soon made glad,
Too easily impressed, she liked whate'er
She looked on, and he was a Man of God.
A trifle short, maybe, and not robust but
The dropping of the daylight at the Manse
Reveals her wisdom. And how know I?
I don't! But I'll take poetic licence if
I choose. Frà Pandolf did and Robert Browning too.
I don't know who she is but if, perchance, you do
Then, let me know and I'll not despatch
My last Duchess to the compost heap
To rest amongst the dead delphiniums.

Mary Rutley

Judy

I had a dog called Judy
a red setter she was.
She had big teeth that everyone
called fangs. She was the best
dog anyone could ever have.
I had her when I was 4. She
died when I was 11. The only
way I didn't take it too
badly was knowing she was
going to heaven. Thank you
Judy for being my best
friend till the end and being
there when I needed a cuddle,
for listening when I cried.
It was a very sad time when
you left us and died.

Raeanne Graefe

Sam

There is beauty in my Collie,
that I've never seen before.
So much love surrounds him,
what has life got in store.

It's got days to remember,
dreams to still come true.
Wrapped around with loyal devotion,
in a love that's pure and true.

Wendy Jackson

The Old Man

(Sadly now deceased 1-4-94) Robert Kerr

Once upon a time, an old man had a stroke,
It was such a shame, as, he was quite a nice bloke.
It left him a shell, of the man he was before,
Which you will find out, as I tell you some more.
He had only one eye and only one hand,
But in his light, I never could stand.
Then along came the stroke, that cut him down,
And it was me, not him, who was wearing the frown.
It affected the side, that had the whole arm,
Fate couldn't have done him, any more harm.
He battled his way through it and recovered a bit,
Though, his arm he lost, the power in it.
His legs were so weak, he couldn't properly walk,
And sometimes, he even struggled to talk.
Didn't complain much and got very thin,
And seemed quite pleased to see me, when I visited him.
Which I did, as often as one can,
How could I not, for that great old man.
All through the years, he'd been, more than bionic,
It would be nearer the truth, if I said, he'd been supersonic.
Believe this if you will, or not, if you'd rather
But, I know it's all true, you see, The Old Man, was my father.

Robert Kerr

Oh! Grandma

Oh! Grandma, not again,
This seems to happen every visit,
You say cheese, I don't know why
And if I smile I'll look exquisite.

Look what's inside that camera thing,
Is that a fly I see in there?
Watch out! It might go up your nose,
Why is your finger in mid-air?

Let's go and play with all my toys,
Do I hear knocking at the door?
Oh! It's my uncle come to visit
Out come the photographs once more.

Iris Hackett

Wild Things

I was once a wild thing
roaming through high grasses
alone and dreaming how I'd fly
far away from my little
iron-fisted town. My lake
glittered with promises,
with wishes I'd send out
in birch-bark canoes.

As a wild thing I say wild things
that make others despair. I walk
now through wet and wildness
as winds batter me. Oh let me be,
let me be left, to find my voice
echoed in birdsong, in roaring
waves of crows that ebb and flow.

I feel your warmth each night,
hear your silent call pressing
against me. You remember my wildness
well, times that drew you in, left you
gasping. Those wild times told you things
you wished would remain unspoken.
To you they were unspeakable.

I burnt a list of unmentionables
on a starless night deep in the wilderness.
In that blaze of light, I saw a path
ahead into forests where wild boar and
gentle deer lived side by side. I lay
on pine needles, watching a full moon rise.
The wild thing was welcomed home at last.

Marianne Nault

Thought Too Loud

(Inspired by Rodin's 'The Thinker')

Was he chained for his thinking?
They took the rest.
Yet; his mind free, rose beyond
The bounds of humanity.
- They tried to hold him captive
  by bonds of conformity -
What was it that filled his head
- It did not work -
  To the point of pausing reality?
- So they tried restraint -
frozen.
- That did not work either -
His life continued on another plane:
Where no-one could reach;
Where no-one could bar;
Where no-one could take away.

Sally Brodie

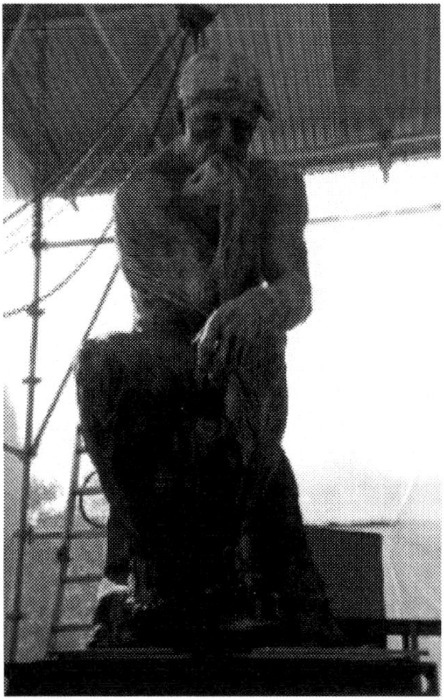

Lasting Friendship

He came to live next door to us
A bright boy with clear blue eyes
Quickly we became firm friends
Much to everyone's surprise

A popular boy, a quiet girl
Sharing hopes, joys and fears
Came the time after graduation
Separation for many years

Happy reunion in familiar places
Cupid smiled from high above
A time of sudden understanding
When lasting friendship turned to love

Flora M Cameron

Dear Mother

Hello Dear Mother how goes life up there today?
I won't keep you long, only a few things to say.
My life is still a mess though I really try,
And since you left I've done nothing but cry!

Mother, Dear Mother I wish you were here,
Instead of being with the 'Master' up there!
I need you more than your 'Father' and his 'Son',
I miss you mother and as for my father I have none!

Mother, Dear Mother you're still my best friend,
You were one in a million and truly a Godsend.
People won't understand this they'll think I'm mad,
Oh Mother this world is just so sad!

Mother, Dear Mother when things get real bad,
I think back to all the good times we had.
The moments we shared, the things we did,
Now more than ever your love I do need.

Mother, Dear Mother how you sheltered me so,
You taught me the things that I now know.
It's true you're not here, we're so far apart,
But you'll be always in my heart!

Mother, Dear Mother you were truly a sweet Mother,
And in this lifetime there can never be another.
Your time and love you would willingly give,
Oh Mother why do you no longer breathe?

Goodbye Dear Mother your time was too short,
Your going has left an aching in my gut!
I would have gone too if I had my own way,
But you're with me each day as I kneel to pray.

Liz Mingo

Sister Sister

(For my precious daughters Kelly and Yvonne)

Together our hearts beat as one
I am the moon you are the sun
Laughing eyes that seem to say
You are the night, I am the day

Locked in a world of pairs and two's
Ticking in time, rhythm and blues
You are the half that makes me whole
My every thought: My very soul

Growing together all through the years
Kissing away each other's tears
You are my shadow as I am yours
Forever a mirror our love ensures

I see myself when I look at you
Have I been: split in two?
The same fair hair, eyes of blue
Where do I end? I wish I knew

Sister, sister, a sweet duet
I am the dawn to your sunset
Side by side our journey begins
Companions for life, next of kin!

Janette B Crawford

Ocean Dining

'Eat me,' the sea lettuce said.
Sumptuously spread, on the sand bed.
So lusciously green, it beckoned me taste.

A spider crab scurrying, spluttering, muttering.
'I'm late, I'm late.' Jellyfish wobbling.
The sun filtering down, a megrim lay smiling.

In Sub Aqua town, purple star fish sated.
I felt so elated, the lettuce posed for a shot.
I snapped it in haste, such a pity to waste.

Mermaids and men, are invited by me.
To come for a nibble, down in the sea.
If you are a conger, you can stay even longer.

Open all hours, the dining hall there.
No need for your wallet, just bring your own air.
You are sure to enjoy, such scumptiousness rare!

Margareth

The Dying Lion Of Lucerne

Proud sits the king of beasts in city squares.
In stone his brothers guard impressive gates,
And rampant stand on many coats of arms.
Courage and strength their symbol indicates.

On columns and on arches lions stare
Unblinking at the populace below,
Fearless defenders of the crown and state,
Aloof and silent let their power show.

Look now upon the 'Lion of Lucerne',
Carved from the rock, he's lying in a cave,
With slackened jaw, head resting on a paw,
And jutting from his side a broken stave.

The pain is there. I feel his agony.
My throat is tight, and tears well in my eyes.
Such suffering I see upon his face,
And, at his helplessness, my spirit cries.

His eyes are barely open. Death is near.
Exhausted now, his consciousness will seep
Down through the solid rock that gave him form.
This noble creature waits eternal sleep.

Patricia Farley

Golgotha. Jerusalem

I walked through the Damascus Gate, outside the city wall,
And faced entranced, that rock the Skull, Golgotha, plain to all.
Golgotha, high above the road, topped by a green grass hill.
I crossed the road and climbed those rocks to the Skull, and time stood still.
I gazed down to the city gate, imagining the cry
From a heartless, cruel, milling mob, the shouts of 'Crucify!'
Christ stumbled past this very scene with lacerated back,
Blood dripping from His crimson wounds from vicious lash attack.
His bruised, tired face so God-like shone, since cruel assault began,
That Pilate was constrained to voice, 'Behold, behold the Man!'

They nailed Him here, in agony, above on that green sward,
Thorn-crowned, scourged and spat upon, they crucified our Lord.
We know He volunteered to come down here on earth to die,
To take our sins upon Himself to shouts of 'Crucify!'
And as I stand here, shaken, moved, never in this way stirred,
I know Christ Jesus is the Lord, I know how true His Word.

Vera Fertash

Autumntide

One day I was strolling along an old country lane
With my two dogs pulling freely on their reins
My thoughts were of the gentle breeze
That lifted and laid a blanket of leaves
In my mind I began to see
Shapes of summer bouquets and Christmas wreaths

Raising my gaze from the ground to the sky
Flocks of migrating birds came fleetingly by
Still looking upwards I observed the naked trees with countless nests
Lots of empty branches the season had undressed

Onwards I ventured into a nearby field
All strewn with straw that the crops did yield
On releasing my dogs from their reins
They ran up and down the field and back again

Soon the sun was sinking down
The sky matched the colours of the leaves on the ground
Hitching up the dogs, back down the lane we proceeded to roam
Seas of confetti remained with us on the long journey home

Michael Monaghan

Feline Contentment

One night in November
We took our maiden queen,
The sweetest girl
We ever had seen.

There followed a time of nuptial bliss
Purrs and caresses, never a hiss!
Our bride returned home; 9 weeks we waited!
The great day arrived just as had been stated.

The kittens popped out - one two and three!
Strong and healthy, a pleasure to see.
Now she shares her kittening pen
With Fleur, her Mum (who'd also had fun!)

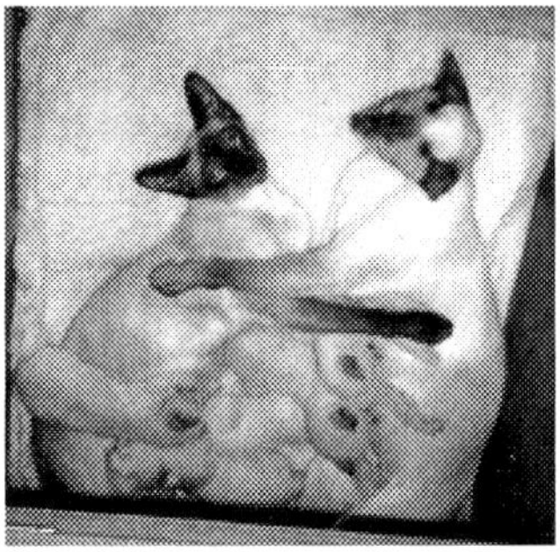

The births were great,
For both Mum and daughter
They each helped one another
As human beings ought to.

They looked after the kittens
They shared the joys
Not caring whether
They'd girls or boys.

A happy contented Siamese Family:
Uncle Ru, Grandma and new Mummy.
They shared in the tasks and basked in contentment
Each helping the other, no show of resentment.

If only humans could copy our Family
And care for and nurture their young so completely.
The kittens: the hub of female domesticity
Harmony, peace and total tranquillity.

Nancy Webster

Young Shoots

They're under my umbrella,
And that's where they will always be.
When rainy days in life appear,
I'm their umbrella tree.

M C Taylor

A Seat, To Lift, To Heaven

A seat, to lift, to heaven

Onwards to nestle in cotton candy clouds made by every daydream.

Higher and higher to transcend from mortal earth, to witness the beauty of nature.

Cradled, safely, to reach the peak, to reach the paradise.

An eagle soaring on wings of a dove, over heaven's whisper.

Lost in serenity in a scenic pasture, graced with divine.

A chair, a moment, a haven.

A seat, to lift, to heaven.

J Cross

Ching-Tzu

Whose funny little face is this looking up at me?
With the softest big brown eyes one could ever see
Who's always there to welcome me when the day is through?
And doesn't lose her temper, no matter what I do
I've never heard her grumble, or even give a snap
I know she never ever would talk behind my back

I know that I can trust her with my very life
Even when I'm feeling down, she won't dig in the knife
So many human friends often let you down
She is the greatest friend I have ever found

What does she ask for all this love that tenderly she gives?
That we stay close together as our lives we live
Then as the years go slowly by together we'll grow old
But we have each other, always close to hold

If ever I should lose her I don't know what I'd do
My gentle faithful little friend that I have called Ching-Tzu.

Dawn Parsons

Only You

And the car alongside
doesn't mean anything,
'cos we posed and pretended
and did silly things,
like buying a postcard
for tenpence, no more,
paddling in waves, up to ankles off-shore
and the blue of your eyes
meant to me more than sea
or sky without clouds
as I daren't say aloud
'bout each thought in my head
making me sort of silly
like first crush at school
but I'm no longer 'Joe Cool'.
So I sit here, pretend,
to look at my shoes
knowing hidden inside me
there is,
only you.

Michael Griffith

Reflections

Life, seen through a
Glass of wine,
Looks fine;
Bathed in a rosy glow,
All worries go;
They fade away,
Until another day;
Right now, who cares?
Let people stare,
It isn't me they see,
Just a parody;
So, for today,
Live life unrestrained,
What is there to be gained
From a broken heart?
Only tears, to start;
So drown your sorrows
In a glass of wine,
And soon you'll find
That life is looking fine!

Dorothy Neil

Holly

My name is Holly and I'm flying high
Up in the trees close to the sky
Hang on called my mistress as I swung on the branch
She grabbed her camera a photo by chance
To please her I stayed swinging to and fro
Wondering which way next I would go
I love it up here there's much I can see
My house mate called Pansy is waiting for me
Right down below a jungle is there
I'm only up here cos I took a dare
I'm loved by my mistress and cared for so well
She ran for a ladder in case I fell
Sometimes I wonder what I used to be
Cos I act like a monkey from tree to tree
I was so tiny and sickly to start
But soon I was to win everyone's heart
I like to be brushed and pampered each day
Cuddled a little and fed the right way
I'm often attacked by the next door cat
I roll on the road on my clean back
Often I eat gnats and chase birds and frogs
I'm so heavy footed it's as if I wear clogs
In the house I sleep on the warmest bed
Stretched out full length looking quite dead
My mistress I have always called mum
When she's around we always have fun
So should you see a cat up a tree
Do look again it could even be me
Please don't worry just leave me there
Cos I'm loved so much by people who care.

Hazel Bowman

From An Oxford Bridge

Leaving the clamour of the bustling city
And Oxford's medieval antiquity,
The country walk provided pleasant contrast,
Sweetness of sound amidst such serenity.

Walking through glades and green meadows,
A warmth in the afternoon sun,
We stood silently on the wooden bridge,
Stillness in the air, not far from your home.

Water flowing quietly beneath the bridge,
Time suddenly at a standstill,
We listened, lost in thoughts of our own,
No ruffle of wind, gazing to Cumnor Hill.

The bridge forged the chasm in our lives,
When at day's end we would part,
Each returning to our own separate world,
But here for a brief moment is my heart.

Linger here in this peace awhile longer,
Preserving the moment deep inside,
Prolong the tremor of happiness within,
Though perfectly calm on the outside.

Under the bridge flow a myriad memories,
Thoughts of that day tinged with joy,
To be added to the store of experience,
Recalled nostalgically as time goes by.

Now when passing by the wooden bridge,
Do you recall in your mind's eye
The splendour of Oxford, of learning,
Revealed to me in that summer gone by?

Betty Mealand

My Dog

My dog is a clown with a permanent frown,
and a heart that's as big as herself,
She is golden in colour with a lovely black mask,
who eventually does whatever I ask.
She adores little children, will stand still for hours
while they hang round her neck, or drape her in flowers.
Most women who come to cuddle her close
are surprised she won't lick, only nuzzle her nose,
She loves to run free for a game in the park,
then chases the Ravens just for a lark.
She follows me close wherever I go,
when she's left alone she makes a big show.
As big as she is she thinks she can sit,
tight up against me half on my hip.
She will lie on her back with her feet in the air
then dives on the bed when I go upstairs.
She's big and she's cuddly and soft as can be,
my wonderful Great Dane that I call Bejay.

Winifred Jenkins

No 9

Sitting it out on a cold lit street
Staring at the stars
Looking for money to prop a bar
Or buy some sympathy

I live at Number Nine
Third box on the right
Don't mind the rats they won't fright
For they also want a bite

People are people so what do you see
When you look at me
Am I the apple of your eye

Watch the boxes move and groan
As you walk down this
Dark lonely crowded street
These boxes with sweaty feet

My bowl is empty the bottle full
That's not how I want it
But now as far as I can see
That's how it's going to be.

Aled Hughes

An Anniversary Poem

It's almost a year, to the day,
That, my granddaughter Chelsea, was taken away.
At the tender age, of only three,
Knocked down by a car, why, did it have to be.
Just outside, her own front door,
Now, I can't see her, any more.
The days they come and the days they pass,
But, I never stop thinking, of that bonnie wee lass.
She was such a little doll,
Loved by everyone, one and all.
But what I miss, most today,
Is, not having wee Chelsea, here to stay.
I know they say, that time will heal,
But no one knows, just how I feel.
All the hurt and all the pain,
No sooner has it gone, then it's back again.
I felt that she, was only mine,
Because, I looked after her, a lot of the time.
But I wouldn't have changed it, not for the finest pearl.
For, she was her Nanna's, Little Girl.

Paddy

Israel Shalom

The sun was shining
Everything went as planned
Here I am
In The Holy Land
My dream came true
In 1993
For the Land of Israel
I always wanted to see
Being half Jewish
On my mother's side
I had a great desire
To see Palestine
Some places I went to
Made me sad
To think of the troubles
The Jews have had
But going on tour
In our air conditioned bus
There were about 20 of us
Welsh, American, Spanish, Chinese
All loving the sights
And the history
Then came the end
Time to come home
I'll never forget you
Israel Shalom.

Christine Williams

Snowdrop

Snowdrop is my lovely cat
and she is almost five,
As her name suggests she is pure white
She is very pretty so healthy, alive.
And loves to cuddle up to me each night.
A very good companion, when
I sit all alone,
Always giving love, which is quite free,
You should see the fuss she
makes when I am on the phone
Trying to make me notice her you see
I am very grateful for my furry little friend
God's special gift that has been sent to me
I shall love and cherish her to the very end
Our partnership was surely meant to be.

Joan Parr Pearse

Polly And Me

Here we go, off again, Polly and me.
Out every day as pleased as can be.
She's in the pushchair, waving arms free,
And I lean on the handle
We're off to the sea.

The wind is sighing, gulls are crying,
Waves are breaking, sandpies we're making
Here we go home again, Polly and me
Always as happy as happy can be.

Trips on the bus, rides on the train,
Over and over and over again
Visits to Morpeth, her cousins to see,
Always as happy as happy can be.

Here we go on again, Polly and me
Off to the church, the people to see
Kneeling in prayer, her little head blessed.
I'm sure she always passes this test.

Skip, hop and jump, together again,
Up on the train and off to see Ben.
Sometimes a teddy, sometimes a doll.
Sometimes she brings nothing at all
Out every day, as pleased as can be
Here we go, home again, Polly and me.

Maisie Bell

Contrary Mary

Little maids in a row for Mary Mary.
Even with their happy, smiles, Mary is still contrary.
Silver bells, ring out in gladness on this happy date
Because the little maids have won first prize at the garden fete.

Weeks they've been planning and sewing.
It has been a busy time preparing
But now it has not been in vain
Today was triumphant, thank goodness it did not rain.

Now, homeward bound, and rather tired
Little maids returning in the van which was hired
Eagerly talking of events of the day,
Planning maybe for next year, come what may

L Culshaw

Our Caravan Holiday

The journey down was slowly,
With hold ups all the way,
We could be rather happy
If the rain would go away.

I've kept my husband busy,
He loves to make the tea,
There's nothing like a cheerful brew
To make the days less drear!

We have been walking daily
In wellies and a mac.
If only soon the sun would shine
We would not hurry back.

But still, we make the best of it,
It's just like 'home from home'!
With tele, knitting, and a book,
All we miss is the phone!

Ruth Lydia Daly

The English Rose

Petals like velvet
With buds tightly formed
Dew shining like diamonds
On each stem adorn.

Fragrantly perfumed
No finer flower grows
Or excels in such beauty
As a True English Rose.

Doris Moss

Suitcase? . . . Nut-Case!

A carousel of luggage
Although mine was never there
On a flight I took to Amsterdam
I was stuck on what to wear
The clothes that I stood up in
Were a little travel weary
So I made the best of what I had
That's my survival theory
I thought of putting on my shirt
A leg thrust in each arm
But I looked quite pornographic
And a sight to cause alarm
I then perused my underpants
But I could only make a hat
And I couldn't go to breakfast
If I was only wearing that
I thought I'd wear a pair of socks
To cover my confusion
But they were bent on slipping off
I was under no delusion
So my brainwave was my toilet-bag
It fitted like a glove
Once I'd shifted soap and aftershave
It only took a shove
And all my precious artefacts
Were packaged out of sight
Though luckily my suitcase
Soon arrived to my delight.

David Whitney

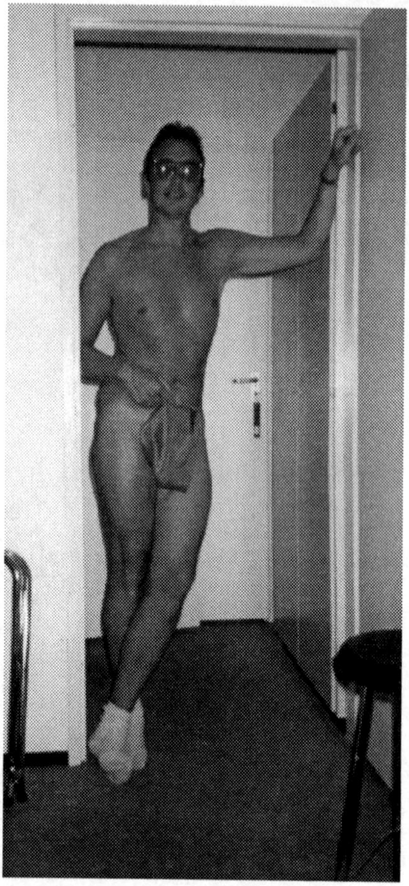

Bare-Faced Cheek

I must call my agent,
how could they be so rude
to omit to tell me
that this ad is in the nude?
I want more money that's for sure,
my mood is getting meaner,
who would think that bearing all
would sell a vacuum cleaner?

Linda Grace

Second To None

They think of rats they think of filth
A vicious dirty sewer scum
I think of you my precious pet
In times of fear to me you'll come
They think of rats they think of cunning
A sleekit creeping thief
I think of you a thief indeed
Intelligence beyond belief
They think of rats they think of evil
Razor teeth with lightning speed
I think of you affectionate friend
The only pal I need
They think of rats they think of germs
Of filth muck and disease
I think of you forever grooming
Immaculate and free of fleas
They think of rats and then they shudder
Vile disgusting creepy one
I think of you and I feel love
My best friend second to none.

Catherine Alderdice

Sea Of Dreams

Close your eyes, imagine the sea,
Inner calm prevails, now you can dream,
Gentle white clouds, the soothing blue sky,
Open your mind to the sea of dreams close by.
Summer sun warming your skin,
Melting away troubles within,
Thoughts float away to let you be,
Allowing you this tranquil dream.
The peace of the ocean stills your life,
On a breeze, a fantasy embraces your mind,
Within a quiet mind, your still body feels no pain,
Only pure thoughts and a content heart remain.
An awareness so clear, no thought can harm,
On the sea of dreams, be peaceful and calm.

Christine Nicholson

My Visitor

I have a visitor
Who I would like you to meet
He visits every morning
To have milk and biscuits with me

He sits on the lawn and watches
Whilst I water my garden patches
He loves the sound of the water hose
Especially when it gets on his nose

He also visits in the night
Putting on my safety light
I always know when he is outside
He wanders far and wide

Chicken is his favourite treat
I love to sit and watch him eat
He has a brush for a tail
It's a lovely fox that is my pal.

Jean Bradbury

Cold Comforter

Summer has flown with the swallows:
Like a red leaf fallen from a tree
Sergeant Major Robin is back,
Ill-mannered, Nazi-tempered
And bristling with self-importance.
    Across the square of lawn
    He parades his obvious contempt
    For feathered gypsies one and all;
    He even insubordinately scolds
    His Excellency, the cat.
That Blackbird over there,
He's big enough
To look after himself. Besides,
He's busy rustling up
A meal in the shrubbery,
Deaf to the world
As he systematically scrapes
And sifts and scrutinises -
You'd think he'd lost a gold eyepiece.
    No bother, Blackbird,
    But I could hate you, Robin,
    If you weren't so funny -
    The way you keep forgetting
    Your cane, your ridiculous obsession
    With Christmas cards,
    And who on earth taught you
    To goose-step
    With both legs at once?

Gordon Booth

Currents At Calvine

I stood under the bridge over the burn,
looked deeply into the clear water
bubbling over brown lichened stones
between peat stained banks and listened
to a multitude of sounds.

I listened in curious, awesome silence,
imagining a hundred tumbling voices
in all inflexions and timbres
talking in changing cadence
rising and falling continuously.

What were they saying to each other?
What news did they animatedly exchange?
Were they ghosts who met on the hills
conversing quickly before dissipating
in the waters of the large river Tay?

Whatever their secrets, I was ignored,
excluded from their constant chatter
leaving me intrigued but no wiser,
yet strangely at peace with currents
of spiritual communications.

M H A Faulkner

Robin Hood Bay September '95

Raging seas,
Endless golden sands,
Steep cliff faces,
Children beachcombing,
Hermit crabs hiding in deep rock pools,
Amongst tangled toothed wrack seaweed,
A glass of chilled lager,
And lunch at The Dolphin.
Strolling hand in hand,
Down snickety winding streets,
Filled with salt worn three storied houses,
Day turns to night,
With cloudless starfilled skies,
The constellations reflecting the dreams,
Of long dead mariners,
Smoke from open fires,
Wafted on the evening breeze,
Heading back to our own cosy cottage,
Creaking floorboards,
And woodworm riddled oak beams,
Steaming hot fish and chips,
In front of a blazing woodburning stove.

Trevor Haith

Put On A Happy Face!

'Deary me.' The fireman said as he waded through the water.
What do I know about compression valves? I can't change a wheel on me car!
He whistled as he chucked out the rugs and smiled, 'sorta'!
'It's only a little flood this, I've been to some real floods in my time,'
I tried to show some enthusiasm but tears choked me, all I could do was mime.
Electric's gone. Carpets gone. The walls had that 'washed' designer look.
Memories of the seaside, Scarbro, Filey came to mind as my rugs they shook.
I made them all a cuppa and gave them home made 'crunch'
The plumber came poured himself some tea through a few 'deary deary me's'
Mug in hand he surveyed the land saying, 'Put on a smile Joyce, there's
Nowt else yer can do? Oh, and by the way, best not use the loo!'
I rang me mum for comfort as tears I couldn't hide,
'A flood! Well aren't you 'gormless, you're like my backside!'
She tutted a lot. Then she laughed, 'Come on love, put on a happy face?'
I'm sick of smiling! I hate the plumber and the firemen! I hate the whole human race!
I'm fed up of trying to win. Of dieting to be thin. Sod it! I'll have a huge chunk of crunchie, get fat, have a double chin!
I kick off me wellies and try to put on a really happy face . . .
To discover there's no more crunchie left in the tin!

J M Hefti-Whitney

Golden Days

Do not despair when life seems bleak
When all is dark and grey
Let each new day be filled with hope
Let sadness melt away
Reach out and take that outstretched hand
For friends are always near
To give support and comfort
To bring laughter, banish fear
Take time to look around you
At the beauty you will see
A rose kissed by the morning dew
Pink cherry blossom tree
The colours of a rainbow
The aureole of the setting sun
Sparkling raindrops clinging
To a web that's just been spun
So fill your heart with sunshine
Walk down the path of promise
For waiting there you soon will find
An everlasting solace.

Audrey Robbins

Joy Before Dawn

Night-time was drawing to a close
as myriads of tiny twinkling stars,
were slowly passing by
they seemed to be sprinkling stardust over the earth.
Or was it my imagination.
While the expectant family, full of mirth,
were anxiously awaiting a phone call,
about a special event, which to them meant
an addition, to our loving circle
A little soul to be loved and cherished
So before the break of dawn, early on Sunday morn.
A baby girl was born (our Megan).
With brown hair, brown eyes, chubby cheeks,
and to little cherry lips, like cupids.
Who could wish for more?

Through her life the sun will rise on high,
in our mighty sky
Warming the earth, which brings forth flowers
of every hue, and roses too.
So we wish her future path to be
strewn with fragrant petals of beauty
and sunshine all the way.

Peggy Johnson

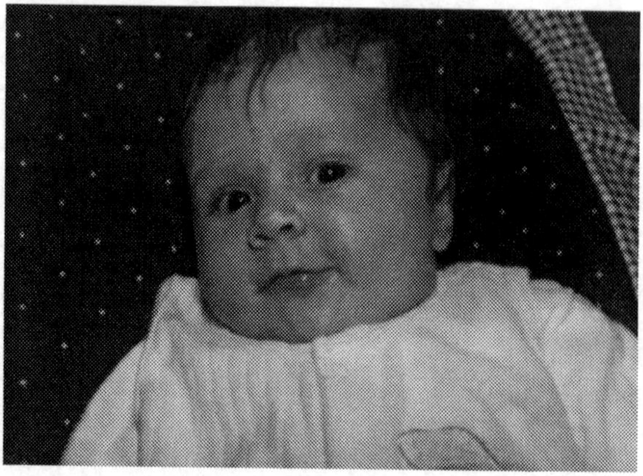

Yesterday

Yesterday saw my eyes fill with tears
Clouding over all of my life's greatest fears
I knows one day there'll be a test of my belief
Pushed to the very edge by an uncertain grief

Life I know must be lived for today
For happiness, can so easily be snatched away
So I take all the love that my daughter gives
She knows that I have doubts, but all of these she forgives

She came to me, for what now seems such a short while
Blesses me every time she gives me her loving smile
My heart is overflowing with her love
I feel that maybe she's an angel sent, from above

My love for her is returned so many fold
That every moment becomes so precious to hold
How can love like this be given so free
That it makes me give a prayer upon bent knee

If time was measured just by only our love
There could be no call to return from above
Memories won't and can't ever possibly replace
The true warmth of her smiling face

If the time should come when we will no longer be
Or the beauty in your smile, again I can never see
You'll live on deep inside of me, you are my very soul
You complete this life, you make me whole

Peter Howarth

My Fair Lady

My Fair Lady was never so fair
As cute and exciting as this little pair
They will tease you, amuse you
And try hard to please you
With their delightful enchanting air
They are always together
Would hate it to part
Now tell me?
Which one has stolen your heart?

Evelyn A Evans

Without You

I am nothing without you,
How often have I heard this said.
But how clear becomes the meaning,
Now that you are dead.

I am only half a person,
Since God took you beyond.
Only half of me is living now,
The other half is gone.

Two springs and one cold winter,
Have passed away with you.
Unnoticed is the sunrise
Or even skies of blue.

I don't remember summer last
Falling leaves at autumn time,
It all fades into nothingness
There is no reason nor rhyme.

The weather is cold today,
Or so I have just been told.
I don't feel any warmth in me,
My heart is ever cold.

Remember how it used to be,
How happy we both were.
Just to be together again,
Is my constant prayer.

We were two halves joined together
How cruel it seems to be,
Why? Oh why? When God took you,
Did he not think of taking me.

Eileen Waldron

The Amaryllis

I had an amaryllis,
    I bought it in a sale.
I watched it grow an inch each day
    With charm that could not fail.

The first bud, as it opened
    Had five flower heads inside,
I watched it daily as it grew
    And opened up with pride.

Then by its side a second bud stood,
    I watched it closely too.
It grew each day much fatter,
    This story I tell to you.

For as it opened daily
    I counted the flower heads new.
Imagine my surprise one day
    When six flowers came to view.

I've never seen such loveliness,
    I'm told it's thirteen years old.
I hope the same for next year
    How could I be so bold?

Margaret E Gaines

The Statue

At Chelsea Flower Show a few years ago,
Some statues I noticed, a lovely show.
A small one I spotted, the size was right,
A graceful girl full of sweetness and light.

Basket in one hand, her arm round a jar,
She calls to mind, sunny countries afar.
I made up my mind, my credit card sought,
Business completed, the statue I'd bought.

Two weeks I waited for delivery time,
Set on a pillar, that statue of mine.
On wintry days she brightens up the scene,
On summer days she's there, cool and serene.

Heather Middleton

It's Four O'Clock, And Time For Tea

It's four o'clock and time for tea,
A bone for you and hay for me.
A pot of tea and a tray of scones,
A definite *must* you must agree!
It's four o'clock and time for tea,
Did I do today? Nothing yet everything.
I ploughed the fields, and I walked with grace,
I watched the happiness that summer brings,
For summer has that curious thirst for thought,
And with it brings such happy times,
For while the cows are a milking,
And the lambs do play,
The cuckoo calls, and the robin sings,
To a gentle rhythm of a welcome stream.
It's four o'clock and time for tea,
A bone for you, and hay for me.'

Jacqueline Humfrey

This Is Me

This is me, aged twenty-three,
During the Second World War.
Our men were abroad. The planes above roared,
We waited and often wept sore.
With dark eyes and hair, so slim and aware
That I had a rather lop-sided smile,
I made all my dresses and brushed my thick tresses,
Was shy, quiet and studious and cycled for many a mile.

I'm not the same me, as at aged twenty-three.
I must say I am very much changed.
My hair somewhat grey, but I'm glad I can say
Thank God that I am not deranged.
I'll be eighty next year, if I'm still with you here
And I try to keep mobile, each day.
I look to the Lord and cannot afford
To forget Him, or stray from His way.
I sometimes feel weak. My bones slip and creak,
But I seek to press on, every day,
I can't do what I would, I only wish that I could,
And that all pains would vanish away.

I'm so thankful to know, that the Lord loves me so
And His miracles have kept me alive.
I must praise Him each day and earnestly pray
That I'll do all I should to survive.
When the trials are o'er and our spirits can soar,
When our dear Lord returns for His own.
New bodies He'll give, for with Him to live
And He promises much joy and a crown.

Winifred R Pettitt

Where The Seals Play

There's a silvery song to the sea where the seals play,
It's a song of the surf and the call of the tide.
And the sands sing their own song as the waves rush away
From the shore, to the sea, to the ocean so wide.

And the seals twist and turn in the sway and the motions,
Diving downwards to caverns on the ocean's deep bed.
It's their home, where they live, and have no fears or notions
Of the killers, of the orcas, which they really should dread.

The waves sing out loudly and sometimes with sweetness
That lulls a seal gently in the swell of the deep.
And the orca has vanished in the ocean's completeness,
And the silvery song is not heard as they sleep.

Pat Hubbard

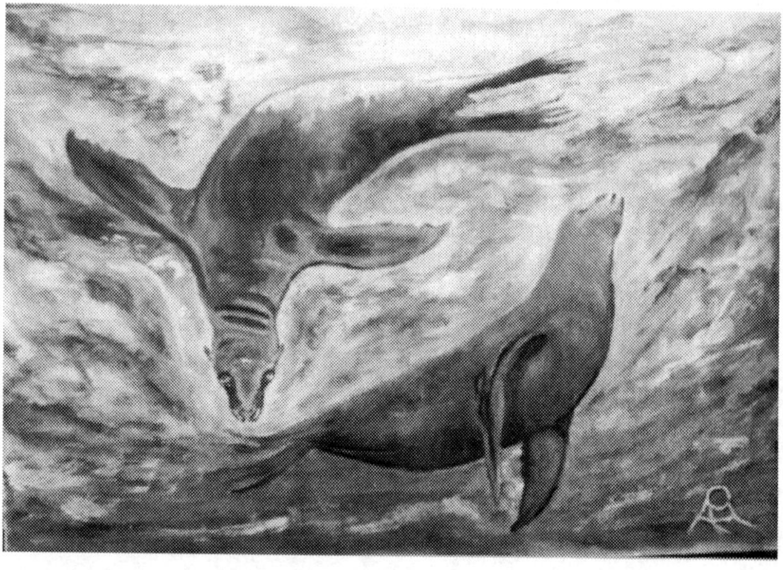

Mountains Of The Sky

When magic waves her slender wand
The flow of pen makes verse a bond
To tie within a matching blend
Of colour's hue as rainbow's end.
With hair so dark and eyes of blue
Her warmth transcends as oceans true.
I dared to hold her near and well
Then felt the measure of her spell.
I rest with visions of her lips
And from her waist of swirling hips
Yet in my sleep her eyes still glint
Revealing some and just a hint
Of tender passions sought to give
Where lies the key to find her heart?
Searching clouds where'er they part
To catch elusive now at last
A moonbeam lit from where 'tis cast.
Dreams that float beyond my sleep
Are silent wishes long and deep
They stay within these realms of mine
The silk and gold make robes of love
A cloak to offer just to one
Who fills my kingdom full of joy
And speeds my sleep with thoughts employ
I cannot hide from all I feel
Nor wish to seem so to conceal
My yearning heart is floating high
Beyond the mountains of the sky.

A J Luke

Town Dwellers

As dusk approaches every day,
In noisy scenes of disarray,
Flocks of countless chirpy fliers
Wheel into town as qualifiers
About to claim their reservations
On Town Hall roofs or railway stations.
Then settle for the long night's wait
Upon each well-selected slate.

In comfort they could roost inside
Lush foliage of the countryside.
But they soldier on under gloomy skies,
Content with hard-to-get supplies.

My leaving town would cause surprise,
So who am I to criticise?

Stanley Longbottom

St David's Day

I hope you think I'm looking sweet,
I'm posing in my Nanna's street,
With bossy sisters dressed to kill,
And me - with just a daffodil!

It's March the first, we shout hooray,
For Wales and for St David's Day,
We eat some Welsh cakes when they're cool,
And then we all go off to school,

Instead of doing sums, we all
Perform a concert in the hall,
I've got to sing a rugby song,
I've practised but I'll get it wrong!

St David, says our Head Miss Grant,
(His name in Welsh is Dewi Sant)
Drank only water, pure and clear,
Not like my father - he drinks beer!

We sing the Anthem, dance about,
We taste a leek, and spit it out,
My sister lets me wear her hat,
And then in Welsh we laugh and chat,

And after lunch, for it's the rule,
They give us half day off from school.
No wonder we all shout and chant
'Three cheers for Wales and Dewi Sant!'

Peter Davies

Laugharne Castle

Those dead grey stony walls
So strongly silent
Ring in the ear of the mind
With medieval pomp and pageant.

Life, love and death have peopled these dead spaces.
The stones dream of their former joy.
No longer post home to some overblown lordling
But fit object for the goggling, gawping know-alls;
'Oh, here is the great hall, there the solar.'

The stones chuckle and laugh to themselves,
Keeping the secrets of past joys in stony silence.

Denys Kendall (Deceased)

My Mother

There is something I would like to tell you, come listen here to me,
Something very special about my Mum and me,
She was a special lady, as special as can be,
I would like everyone to know how much she meant to me.
When I was just a baby, a baby upon her knee,
She loved me oh! so very much and she meant the world to me,
But the years went by and I grew up and still she cared for me,
Then one day my Mum was gone, and life just changed for me,
No last goodbye no fond caress, so-special smile I see,
I know you watch me from above and guide me in all I do,
Oh! what I would give my darling mother for yesterday and you.

Betty Walker

Rudy And The Shells

Rudy said the sea has many artists,
Who decorate the shells beneath the waves.
Their colours are so vivid, their patterns beautiful,
My friend collected them and cleaned them
And strung the shells together for a necklace.

These days I see art in everything.
I watch God's hands careful and small
Paint the skies in glorious blues and golds.
He sculpts the stubborn rocks, encourages
Mighty tides to break upon the shore,
He collects men's hearts like shells and cleans them,
And strings our souls like pearls across his kingdom.

Keith Wright

Fistral

I had a dream . . . not of Manderley
But of a beach not far away
A perfect scenario of romance not Figaro
Of seals and sunsets and rolling waves
Red skies and barbecue fiascos
Lovers relaxing, seabirds diving
Folk conversing about sea and fun
Cares of life forgotten, until the sun
Sets against an azure sky above
How glad I am to live here on this, our Earth.

Linda Guest

Viewing The Taddei Tondo

(Michelangelo Buonarroti, The Royal Academy)

It's obvious half realisation
is more fascinating, enigmatic
than bold, bezelled actualisation.
We've climbed vitreous steps, automatic
in our assumption they will bear our weight,
and now stand face to face with Christ, St John.
The babe recoils from His prefigured fate.
A goldfinch holds their-and our-attention.
This is that same bird whose blasphemous theft
of berries from Messiah's thorny crown
drew scarlet beads from His brow. All this left
to our imagination and not shown:
a veil not dragged right back, but partly drawn.
And marble's own epiphany, éclat
provides the nimbus we rely upon,
hallowing all with a magnificat.
We seem to stand upon mere reflection;
art aiding in us the visionary,
summoning faith in His resurrection:
elevation from the ordinary.
Our souls are gradually teased, released
as we feel translucence behind stone's chill.
In a blink we find wonders haven't ceased
and the master chisel is not yet still.
Like struggling slave figures in Florence
who grapple to achieve transformation
from half-hewn blocks, seeking deliverance
our striving eases in adoration.
Contemplating heaven with feet of clay
we find relief; moulds break and fall away.

Marion Primrose

You And Me

Let's get together
that's what friends are for
I'll give you a drink of mine
if you give me some of yours
then we will get merry
happy we'll both be
always sharing and caring
always together
you and me.

Kenny Dunn-Fox from Leek

Blossom

We hopefully believe you'll come again
Gracing the riverside and down the lane
As year by year, O faithful lovely tree
Your beauty skirts the place with loyalty.
Open to all and free is your fair spread
As Hawthorn blossom hangs from overhead
And all her pretty cousins take her lead
As one by one they flower o'er Fenland mead.
The laden boughs in varying size and shapes
Take on the form that only Nature drapes
Upon each hedge and tree around the land
Pink or pure white, for our delight they stand.
So Lincolnshire is dazzling to behold
As the gorgeous blossoms now unfold
Clothing the edge of our acres wide
A common sight by the field's side.

Mary Waters

A Cold Winter's Day

The bitter air, and watery sky,
Frost-bitten trees, they moan nearby,
The icy ponds, and frozen streams,
Their once warm waters, make chilly screams,
The glistening hills, fields, and greens,
Their once lush textures, cannot be seen,
Enchanced with snow, and ice, and frost,
Their well known features, look almost lost,
The hot warm sun, seems far away,
It certainly is, a cold winter's day.

Christopher A J Evans

Fat Cats!

We really take exception
to the terms you humans use.
It is quite a wrong deception
when you want to hurl abuse -
To link us up with greediness
is really quite absurd -
Just because our paws like creaminess
and we are softly furred.
We are loved by millions
for our sweet and loving ways -
Not for piling up some billions
and making other pussies strays!
We really, must request you now
not to include *us* in your sins,
We are not fat pussy cats
with ugly Cheshire grins.

Betty Wilson

Yesterday's Childhood

In a sleepy little town hidden from view, with your
crumbling plaster and paint far from new
there stands my memories of childhood gone, untouched
by the years as they roll on
every room the same as I remember suspended in time
as I drift along, a curtain from long ago draws back
in my mind
The winding stairs, the old dark attic, shadows from
the past brush my cheek and make me gasp
My Mother's lovely face shines through the gloom,
I sense her presence as I drift from room to room
The faint smell of lavender embraces me, I close my
eyes and tears begin to loom
Where Christmas trees and lights once stood and
children laughed, now in its place an empty room
that keeps its secrets in the gloom
The old kitchen with its blackened range, where feasts
for Kings were often made, its aroma held a spell
no-one could break.
An overgrown garden thick and dense, a broken swing
a rotten fence
A thousand memories lingering on, drifting in my
head like a haunting song, a wonderful childhood
gone for so long.

Carol Irving

My Sister's Firstborn - Jack

A new life unfurled
Screaming, fearing the unknown.
Scrumpled and blotchy
Beautifully formed and ungrown
Amazing and more amazing
This phenomenon is to me
So precious, so vulnerable
So responsive to Zeem
Such basic requirements
Wee pruneface demands
But utterly consuming
A breast and four hands!
Love, warmth and food
It's not much to ask
It's merely a 24 hour day task!
The power of small lungs
The power of his cry
His red walnut face
That demands prompt reply.
I love little Jack
His life is incredulous
It's simply astounding
However in readiness
The scent of his skin
The curl of his lip
His wrinkly wee hands
His powerful grip.
Those dark, watchful eyes so full of expression
Within moments of life, he made his impression.

Sara-Jane Sheikh

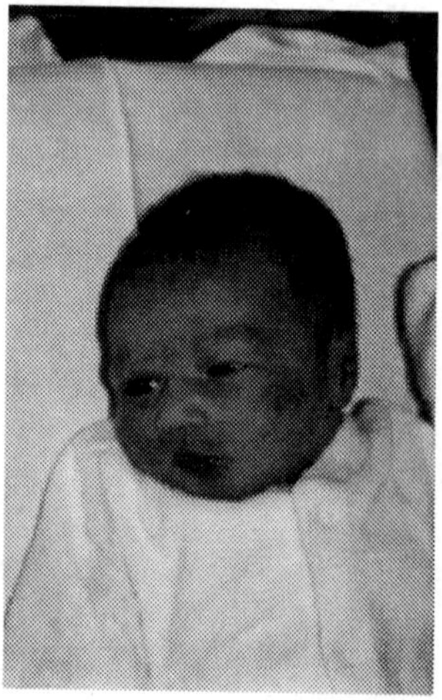

Freak

They stare at me and start to snigger,
Just because they are slim and I am bigger,
Feeling hurt once again inside,
I hurry home to my room and hide,
Tears of shame roll down my face,
Am I really such an ugly disgrace?
But as the hurt takes over
A voice says to me,
'You are kind like everyone,
Should be'
You care and have respect,
They don't, you recollect,
So it's them who are the freaks,
Cold-hearted people in the street.

Claire Young

Sally

I just wanted to tell you about our Sal,
A very fine dog and a great little pal.
Once you have a dog it is never the same,
Lots of the unexpected, much love, some pain.

Jabs at the vet, paper on the floor,
A squeaky, fluffy puppy, waiting by the door.
The first time she found her voice, a brand new bark;
She showed it off to brother Tom when out in the park.

So clean and understanding everything that's said
The bedroom door, left just open, so up onto the bed
For a quick nap after lunch, to be rested for the greeting
Of family coming home at the end of the evening.

For years she was always there, in her favourite places;
On the landing, in the garden, lots of cat chases.
Gradually becoming slower, and not as much care,
Wobbly on those older legs, but the will is still there.

As I held her in my arms as I had often done,
And carried her to the car for a ride in the sun.
Just before Christmas she barked her last,
Only a small one, a reminder of the past.

After 20 years she is there still
In our memories she always will
Be on that chair or in that part
Of the park or watching the sky as it becomes dark.

Was that her by the door, out the corner of my eye?
No, just my old boots, in her favourite spot, I begin to cry.
A love that lasted so many years still grows and still grows,
Sally - how we shall all miss you so.

Phyllis O'Connell